THE EVIL EXECUTIVE

THE EVIL EXECUTIVE

Encounters with malicious and abusive behaviour in the workplace

SIMON MAIER

Marshall Cavendish Business

Published by Marshall Cavendish Business
An imprint of Marshall Cavendish International
1 New Industrial Road, Singapore 536196

Other Marshall Cavendish Offices:
Marshall Cavendish Corporation. 99 White Plains Road, Tarrytown NY 10591-9001, USA • Marshall Cavendish International (Thailand) Co Ltd. 253 Asoke, 12th Flr, Sukhumvit 21 Road, Klongtoey Nua, Wattana, Bangkok 10110, Thailand • Marshall Cavendish (Malaysia) Sdn Bhd, Times Subang, Lot 46, Subang Hi-Tech Industrial Park, Batu Tiga, 40000 Shah Alam, Selangor Darul Ehsan, Malaysia

Marshall Cavendish is a trademark of Times Publishing Limited

National Library Board Singapore Cataloguing in Publication Data:
Name(s): Maier, Simon.
Title: The evil executive : encounters with malicious and abusive behaviour in the workplace / Simon Maier.
Description: Singapore : Marshall Cavendish Business, [2016]
Identifier(s): OCN 953678852 | ISBN 978-981-47-2115-8 (paperback)
Subject(s): LCSH: Bullying in the workplace–Prevention | Racism in the workplace–Prevention. | Abuse of administrative power–Prevention. | Personnel management. | Communication in management.
Classification: DDC 658.382–dc23

Design by Bernard Go Kwang Meng

Printed in Singapore by JCS Digital Solutions Pte Ltd

Dedicated to the victims of evil people – not only the victims I've met, but those many, many whom I haven't

Hell is empty,
All the devils are here.

The Tempest, Act I, Scene 2

CONTENTS

INTRODUCTION

> And in my voice
> most welcome shall you be
>
> *As You Like It*, Act II, Scene 4

We all probably know someone, in authority or otherwise, who has at one time or another bullied us. That's not uncommon—from the sibling at home to the thug in the playground to the manager at work who is extremely unpleasant on a regular basis and has a bunch of acolytes who are co-bullies. Sometimes we can stand up to these people; sometimes we can get support from those around us—our parents, other siblings, our boss, our friends, sometimes our HR departments, our unions or the law. Sometimes we do nothing, whether out of shame, fear or simply helplessness. Sometimes the results are severe and painful in all sorts of ways. Bullying of any kind is nasty, often long-lasting—even once it has stopped—and can cause huge problems at later stages in our lives, no matter how old we are. And this can occur socially, at home or at work. Anywhere.

Bullying is one thing, but it can go a stage further and manifest itself as something that warrants the word 'evil'.

This is when someone in authority—or even an associate, colleague or peer—causes real, lasting damage, physical or mental (or both), to those with whom they work. The line between bullying and evil can be thin and there is often no real demarcation, just levels of pain caused.

This is a universal issue. Evil is not limited by class, creed, money, position, sex, nationality, faith, size or age. There are managers in the world of business and politics, in education, in the service industries, in construction, in factories, in the high street and in the shopping malls—indeed, in all walks of life—who are psychotic, willing to cause extreme distress and who are able to manipulate people, harm them with impunity, cheat and lie.

Evil executives find their way into corporate, political and organizational life easily. As job candidates, they are able to project candour, trust and complete worthiness. They are often very good actors. They can dissemble. They may, indeed, have done well in their own right academically or on the back of others and they may be regarded within their professions as brilliant, honourable, a safe pair of hands and successful. Sometimes these people get away with their ghastliness. Sometimes they are exposed. In every case, they cause damage.

Have no doubt—these people are monsters. This may sound like hyperbole, but it really isn't. These directors, managers and front-line supervisors can turn a productive workplace into a morass of hate and fear. They make working life truly miserable, resulting in less engagement, lower job satisfaction, fading morale, increased absenteeism, physical illness, mental stress and, occasionally, even death.

Moreover, monsters at work can wreak legal havoc for a company, causing bad publicity and tainting its brand image. This usually occurs when workers, victimized by brutish bosses, go public because they just can't take any more abuse. Or it occurs when the media discovers what's going on and opens up the can of worms. Or, indeed, it occurs when a business goes bust or when it's discovered that someone at the very top has been using an organization illegally or immorally for huge personal gain.

Exposure, though, doesn't occur enough. Evil executives are not always easy to spot; or, if they are, they are certainly not easy to stop or challenge. Often the victim is isolated and has only a small voice or none at all. Or the victim is unable to do anything, having become a nervous wreck. Usually, the victims suffer, leave and, maybe, just maybe, die in silence.

Although most good quality and well-managed organizations foster positive environments on a macro level, it's likely that at least a few mid-level toxic managers are causing terrible problems at the micro level. That is, behind the scenes and without the knowledge of people at the very top. Evil executives can often be malicious, vicious, insidious or draconian in their actions towards targeted employees. They isolate staff, then divide and conquer by targeting certain workers for abuse and others for favouritism. The focus is often based on non-job-related factors. And once the target is in their grasp, they seldom let go.

Evil executives might damage staff with an abundance of malice under the guise of micromanagement. They use multiple fear tactics, including, but not limited to, intimidating employees with frequent, shouted verbal outbursts ridden with expletives and crude physical gestures. They humiliate victims by demeaning them during meetings or in front of co-workers. They may constantly look over their target's shoulders, literally and figuratively, for the smallest mistake or excuse to castigate them (sometimes with violence). They set impossible-to-complete assignments and laborious administrative tasks on even senior employees. They will do anything to strengthen their own position and maintain power.

Such manoeuvres eviscerate any semblance of employee motivation, job satisfaction and organizational loyalty. Evil executives make environments dangerous places for their victims and colleagues, resulting in lower overall performance by individuals and teams—which negatively impacts a company's bottom-line results or an organization's output. People who are sad, wretched and frightened are unlikely ever to be a good face for any organization. The fact that senior management and external parties may close their eyes to this picture doesn't make the picture acceptable. But accepted it mostly is.

Chances are you know people who just don't seem to play by the same rules as everyone else, who are happy to manipulate, who enjoy hurting people, who discard others and who say or do anything to protect their own image or reputation, while at the same time doing nothing to protect the values and vision of the organization they work for or their colleagues.

Knowing something about how these personalities function, what motivates them, and how they behave is essential for your personal resilience at work. Evil executives thrive on harassment and discrimination in order to get their own way, to hurt (because they can), and to prove that they have power (because they do). They may harbour racist, sexist, ageist or homophobic views that become manifest within the office setting. They get away with it and so can do it some more. They may target innocent and hard-working people based on any factor: disability, age, colour, religion, ethnicity, gender, size, shape, sexual orientation, pregnancy, walking in a particular way, a stutter, size of nose and so on. Such executives might sexually harass female or male employees, both verbally and physically. And we're not talking about minor infringements here; this can be constant or it can be a drip feed over months and years.

If all of that isn't bad enough, such evil executives often resort to knee-jerk reactions and retaliate against targeted victims who speak out or begin to exercise their rights. They are clever. They will know how to use rules for their own purposes. They will tie their targets in knots. And, if they don't, then they have acolytes who will do their bidding in a heartbeat.

The evil executive usually favours, mentors and promotes only selected staff based on personal loyalty. This is gangland by another name. Even in a diverse organization, small or large, some bigoted managers might use racial, ethnic and sexist slurs to harass employees behind closed doors—and then pretend that all is sweetness and light once 'out in the open'. They could on the whole behave brilliantly well, particularly in front of senior staff. But victims know that the smiles change to snarls and the softness turns to violence. Employees who are subjected to such discriminatory tactics often dread going to work and are prevented by the evil executive from working or behaving properly—and that in turn creates a vicious circle. The result is an atmosphere of sheer terror and perpetual unease—in short, hell. This, then, is evil at work.

Toxic personalities are people who demonstrate a pattern of counter-productive behaviour that is debilitating not only to their victim, but also to other people in the vicinity. However, in order to apply the label 'toxic', these behaviours have to be pervasive. They have the potential to cause serious damage to people, property or the fabric of a workplace—whether a corner shop with three people working in it or a multi-national employing 300,000.

Another very important factor to consider is that investigations into terrible behaviour are rare. Even when they do occur, while any investigation is taking place—often over months and sometimes years—the evil continues and can indeed increase. The same can be said when there are wider social or organizational difficulties not necessarily caused by the evil executive. This is borne out in economic downturns or when a business or organization is in some difficulty; then the 'shadow' side of people's personalities can emerge and toxicity spreads like a nasty virus. It becomes a contagion. The contagion is then seized upon by those who have low morals or who are psychotic by nature—and they then spread the contagion. This is possibly a version of the 'I was only obeying orders' theme. Suddenly, any empathy with the decency in people diminishes or disappears.

Lack of empathy is the root cause of most evil at work. Empathy is the ability to identify what someone else is thinking and feeling and to respond to their thoughts or feelings with an appropriate emotion, such as kindness. If we lose empathy, then we become lost as decent people. But this is not to say that everyone is likely to be evil if the circumstances are virulent. Most people are decent. Most people will speak up for what is right. Most people will fight for injustice and against violence. The problem is that it is very hard to fight within a toxic environment.

Very senior managers often support the toxic executive. They may welcome him or her as one of their own kind. They may admire many 'qualities' that they assume are related to achievement—making money, sorting out organizational problems, pushing processes to the edge, breaking rules to save time, effort and costs, and so on. Once a toxic personality becomes part of the management group, it takes a near disaster to weaken his or her power.

If anyone threatens the toxic individual, management might close ranks and, if someone complains about the toxicity, the management team may then treat that complainant as the problem.

So, who do we think of in the context of an evil executive? Do we include people who work in organizations you know? Do we include famous examples of white-collar crime and fraud, such as Dennis Kozlowski, who eventually rose to the position of CEO with Tyco and who allegedly siphoned off $600 million in company funds for his own use? His excesses were said to include $6,000 shower curtains, lavish parties at the company's expense and false bonuses he claimed were approved by the board of directors. Kozlowski served a prison sentence and lost everything. Do we mean him?

Or do we think of Richard Scrushy's alleged evil practices while in charge of HealthSouth Corporation? He was twice charged with 30 counts of illegal practices while acting as CEO. His crimes are said to include authorizing the termination of whistleblowers. Yes, termination. He was also accused of bribery, fraudulent accounting practices, extortion, money laundering and mail fraud, among many other felonies. Although he managed to avoid jail in 2003, he was later convicted on 30 different charges in 2007 and sentenced to six years and 10 months in prison. HealthSouth survived Scrushy's abuses. Do we mean him?

What about Robert Maxwell, who ran a huge publishing and media empire, often with alleged menaces and possibly worse? Maxwell died mysteriously at sea in 1991.

His death triggered the collapse of his publishing empire as banks called in loans. News emerged that Maxwell had apparently stolen hundreds of millions of pounds from his own companies' pension funds. The Maxwell companies applied for bankruptcy protection in 1992. Do we mean people like him?

And then there's Enron, which became a huge global story. As a big power player at Enron, Chairman Jeffrey Skilling encouraged the questionable accounting tactic known as mark-to-market. It allowed the business to estimate overly optimistic values for energy prices by appraising company holdings based upon expected values. Skilling also signed off on the creation of an Enron subsidiary called Chewco, which was little more than a dumping ground for Enron's debt. Skilling was sentenced to 24 years and four months in prison. The business eventually collapsed, taking with it the jobs and life savings of thousands of employees.

There are many instances where organizations are said to practise evil. Take this example. Sam Walton and his brother founded Wal-Mart in 1962 and today that company is one of the largest private employers in the world, as well as one of the largest retailers in the world. Wal-Mart is often accused of treating employees like a commodity—and no incident possibly proves this more that than the case of 52-year-old Debbie Shank. After becoming paralysed in a collision, Shank's family was apparently awarded $700,000 in damages. After legal fees were paid, $417,000 was placed in a trust to pay for Debbie's long-term care. But it is said that Wal-Mart had paid out about $470,000 for Shank's medical expenses and later sued for the same amount—because her employment contract seemingly stipulated that any damages won by an employee were the property of the company. Is this evil or just 'rules'?

There are instances of evil in all kinds of organizations, little and large, throughout history. Remember that an organization only practises evil because those within it allow it to happen. Hermann von Siemens was the CEO of Siemens during World War II. Before the war, Siemens was a major player in helping the Nazi party to rebuild the German army, improve infrastructure and eventually help put in place the mechanisms that drove the Holocaust. During the war, the company's acts included operating factories at the infamous concentration camps of Auschwitz and Buchenwald. Jewish slave labour was used in those factories to create electrical switches for military use. Those same slave labourers would later meet a terrible end inside Siemens-built gas chambers operated at both camps.

Evil can exist anywhere where someone can freely hurt people and damage their lives by pursuing their own ends with impunity. Someone said in a meeting I attended recently, 'If you are not a predator, you will become someone's prey.' Is that true, do you suppose? And Einstein wrote, 'The world is a dangerous place to live; not because of the people who are evil, but because of the people who don't do anything about it.' I am very afraid that this *is* true.

PART ONE

EVIL AT WORK

The following are case-study interviews with people who were, or are, victims of evil in the workplace. Each situation is different and they all have some common ground. In one instance the interview is with an evil executive.

The examples are deliberately broad in choice and scope. There are some where the evil executives are hidden or are part of a huge conspiracy at which nobody can point a finger. In many of the examples it is not always clear to see how the victims could defend themselves against—or, indeed, readily recognize—someone with a personality disorder that manifests itself in terrifying and damaging antisocial behaviour that is redolent of true evil.

01

SUSAN, COMMUNITY SERVICES CASEWORKER
MANCHESTER, UK

> Well, everyone can master a grief
> but he who has it.
>
> *Much Ado About Nothing*, Act III, Scene 2

"Shall I sit here? Thanks. OK. Where to start?

I was a community services caseworker who had been newly employed in a suburban community services office. You'll have to forgive my stutter. I'm sorry... No, no. That's fine. Well… well, prior to obtaining tertiary qualifications for this work, I'd had a number of caseworker jobs. I was... happily married with two children… No, it's fine. I'm OK. Sorry… give me a moment.

My supervisor, Wendy, was very helpful to me for the first six months of my employment and commended me on several occasions for my work. She was beautiful—really attractive and always well turned out. Wendy also had very good relations with other staff members, although she had told me, just after I started, to have as little as possible to do with another caseworker, Margaret, because she was what Wendy called a 'troublemaker'.

A few weeks after starting work, I kept finding Wendy looking at me—staring. That was unnerving. Then, soon after that, she would occasionally brush softly against me and touch my arm or shoulder unnecessarily. Late one afternoon, alone in an office, I turned to find her standing behind me. She kissed me... on the mouth... and I was so shocked I didn't react immediately. Well, to cut a long story short, we had a brief dalliance—not sleeping together but kissing, hugs, small presents, some lunches, dinners and a couple of long walks holding hands—that sort of thing. I had never been attracted like that to another woman, but my marriage was going through a rocky patch and, well, I found Wendy attractive and she was attracted to me. It was flattering. It was reassuring and I liked it. But clearly Wendy was very keen to take it to the next level, despite the fact that she knew I was married with a family... Look, I was confused. I liked her affection and actually, well, I wanted to have sex with her.

About a month later, Wendy gave me a file concerning a department client. She explained that she had been working with the client for several months, but wanted me to get some additional experience by dealing with that particular client. I was really pleased. I thought that I'd made the grade.

I went through the file and Wendy's file notes. As I read, it became very clear to me that Wendy hadn't followed proper departmental procedures. In fact, she had clearly cut corners and had been completely unprofessional. This was confirmed when I met with the client a week later.

I thought about this a lot and it really worried me. How should I proceed? I believed that the best way of dealing with the issue was to directly express my concerns to Wendy with the view of clearing up any possible misunderstandings… and I was sure that there would be a straightforward explanation. However, Wendy's reaction to my concerns was extremely cool—icy—and she demanded the return of the file. Her attitude towards me totally changed from that moment on. I mean *really* changed.

In the following weeks and months, my appearance, my clothes, the way I did anything (including how I blew my nose when I had a cold) and my work performance became the subject for criticism. I'm attractive, I think—well, people say so—but she made every effort to criticize my looks and my clothes, often in front of co-workers. She would exclude me from any group discussion and twice deliberately didn't invite me to departmental meetings. Then, one afternoon she pushed me hard in a car parking bay, so that I tripped and badly cut my knee. She helped me up and said it was an accident, but it wasn't. And she was smiling. A smug smile.

On another day we were both making coffee in the office and she was seemingly pleasant. Suddenly she tipped a mug of scalding coffee over my left arm. Again, she apologized, said it was an accident, but I could tell that it wasn't and that she was pleased. The burns were really painful and I had to have medical care.

In the end, I approached Margaret, a timid woman, who, after some persuasion, revealed that she had been through a similar experience with Wendy, but was not sure how to handle her. She was terrified of talking about Wendy and had been told that if she, Margaret, ever breathed a word, she'd be fired with a really bad reference. Margaret said that Wendy could become extremely abusive and violent if she didn't get her own way. I was angry that Margaret hadn't said anything before now, although really I was angry with myself.

I spoke to our union organizer about the issue, who suggested that at the next regional union meeting he would raise my complaint with members. I was very nervous and worried that I had done the wrong thing. What if the union guy talked to Wendy? What if they supported each other? Well, the union meeting's time was dominated by discussion of this issue. Wendy wasn't a union member, so she wasn't there—thankfully. Without naming Wendy, Margaret, along with myself and two other workers, all recounted much the same experiences. Apparently, some of Wendy's behaviour had been violent. Physically violent. This prompted a couple of clerical staff to recount their own experiences about her. One of these people informed the meeting that she was receiving psychiatric treatment as a result of what Wendy had allegedly done at work.

The meeting passed several resolutions in relation to violence that were to be sent on to management. The union also provided a number of posters on the subject of workplace violence, which were put up around the office. All of the posters disappeared overnight but the union delegate replaced these the following day. Wendy's attitude towards me became vitriolic. She ensured that my husband knew about our 'relationship' and not that long afterwards he left home with the children. We're separated now… probably going to be divorced, yes. I'm on all sorts of medication for depression.

Wendy continued to make life very hard for me—making me work late, making me miss appointments, losing documents that I knew I'd given her, not signing forms, marking me down for taking leave when I was actually at work, humiliating me in public, laughing at me openly—things that made me feel I was going mad. And then, occasionally, she'd be very kind and helpful, only to lure me into a false sense of security before she reverted to type and became aggressive and, well, an enemy.

I've left the organization now, but she hasn't."

02

ANNA, CHILD PROTECTION OFFICER
LONDON, UK

> A glooming peace this morning with it brings. The sun, for sorrow, will not show his head. Go hence, to have more talk of these sad things
>
> *Romeo and Juliet*, Act V, Scene 3

"Good morning. Hello, I'm Anna. Shall we start? OK, so... Let's see...

Well, I was employed in a regional child protection unit. My job involved removing children from families in situations where there was evidence of physical or sexual abuse—all too frequent, I'm afraid. I was often used for this work where local families were involved. My background and ethnicity helped.

The department's procedures involving this type of work required two child protection staff and at least one police officer to be involved in removing a child. Those rules are golden. Well, they were.

A new manager, Ian, had been appointed in charge of the unit. He'd been transferred as a promotion to this role. To start with, the relationship between Ian and the whole unit was cool. Cool as in a cold way, not a good way. He wasn't particularly friendly, never smiled and assumed that everyone would work his way. There was an immediate tension whenever he walked into a room.

Early on a Friday afternoon, Ian told me that the unit was going to remove a child from a family as a result of alleged physical abuse and neglect. Ian told me that he planned to carry out the task later in the afternoon. The family in question lived in a motor home in a local caravan park.

I told Ian that I had had previous experience with that particular family and confirmed that there was a history of alcohol abuse and domestic violence. I also told him that on the last occasion I had contact with the family, the father of the child had physically threatened me. Ian's response was: 'Well, it goes with the job, so let's not make a fuss...'

When we arrived at the caravan site later that afternoon, I asked Ian when the police were likely to arrive. Ian told me irritably that he hadn't requested police assistance and told me to focus on the job rather than make what he called 'bloody stupid suggestions'. I said to Ian that I wasn't prepared to take a child into custody without police assistance, since it was contrary to departmental procedures—and I had fears for my own safety from previous experience with the family. Ian became extremely angry indeed and told me, actually shouted at me, spitting in my face, that if I refused to assist him he would have me disciplined. I was shocked and frightened. Local people were watching and the situation was becoming very tense. I agreed to assist Ian.

When Ian and I informed the parents of the child of the purpose of our visit, both parents became extremely violent and physically assaulted first Ian and then me. I don't know if you've seen violence at close quarters starting from nothing, but I promise you it's terrifying. Absolutely terrifying. Ian had a broken nose and a nasty cut above an eye. It all happened very quickly. I had deep scratches to my face and arms, a deep cut on my forehead and a broken finger. The parents literally threw us out of the caravan and locked the door. I tripped on a step and cracked a tooth. There was blood everywhere. Ian made no effort to help me. However, he did then call for police assistance, with three officers arriving 10 minutes later. The police arrested the parents after they attempted to assault the officers and the child was taken into custody.

I didn't want to go back to the office with Ian and, anyway, I thought we both needed to go to hospital. The police offered me a lift, sensing my discomfort, and I think I was crying as well, but Ian waved the police away and said that he'd take care of me. On the way back to the office, in his car, Ian told me that if I reported him for failing to use departmental procedures he would hurt me. He snarled as he said this. I said nothing, but I started to cry again and my cuts were bleeding, my broken finger was swollen and I felt very faint. He repeated what he'd said, shouting obscenities and demanding that I told him that I'd understood. I said that I needed a doctor and asked to be dropped off at a hospital. He refused.

People were shocked when we got back to the office. A colleague took me to hospital and I think that Ian went home. I was off work for several weeks as a result of the physical injuries I received and the emotional trauma arising out of the violent confrontation with the child's parents, not to say my utter terror of Ian. I didn't want to go back to work, but I did.

When I did go back, I found that my colleagues were very distant with me. Within 15 or so minutes, Ian called me into his office, locked the door and said, 'Have you had any thoughts about what I said to you when we were coming back to the office after that job we did together?' I replied that I had not made up my mind about it.

Ian yelled, 'Well, let me tell you, you disgusting piece of crap, that you have one day to make up your mind, otherwise you're going to be in serious trouble. I'm not joking. I hope that you're very clear on this!'

I said, 'I'm not the one who'll be in trouble. You will be. You're the one who didn't follow procedures and you shouted and bullied me—and stopped me going straight to hospital. And you refused to call the police in to assist, when you should have.'

Ian interrupted, 'Oh really? So, we'll see what happens if you say a word against me. I will get you, you cow. You'll always be looking over your shoulder.'

I didn't say anything, but he ranted on. 'All you do is whine. You should hear yourself. I've already covered what happened—in considerable detail—in my report on the incident so, if you say something different, you're going to be in big trouble, not me, sunshine. Do you understand? And everyone in the office knows that you're rubbish!' He spat the words and I could see venom in his face, real hate.

I got up and tried to leave his office. He came to the door and grabbed my shoulders and shook me violently. 'If you don't do the right thing you ******g black bitch, I'll bloody get you. You'll be sorry. And without a ******g job!' Then he unlocked the door and pushed me out hard.

I was shocked and trembling. I went home. Next day I decided to get some advice from a friend. He said that the best idea would be to lodge a formal grievance in writing and send it to my regional director. I forwarded the grievance the same day.

The department's grievance policy required that the regional director contact me within seven days. After a month, I hadn't heard anything and was going to call the director when I received a letter from her directing me to transfer to a position some hundred miles away at another office within six weeks. I was stunned. Absolutely stunned. This would impact on my own family and financial circumstances, as I had just bought a flat only in the past year.

I met my friend Pete, who's a lawyer. I'd found out that Ian had told people that he had been put at risk by me on the day of the incident with the family from which we'd removed a child, as I had refused to help him take the child into custody when the police were not available. He claimed to have asked for police assistance. I told Pete my version of events, which was verified by the local police with a phone call.

I asked to meet Ian with Pete, as my lawyer. He refused, but changed his mind when I emailed to say that I would go to the police. The meeting was attended by someone from HR; it was an acrimonious meeting and not at all helpful. Ian wouldn't change his story—that is, tell the truth—and he tried to make out that I was unprofessional and that it was me who hadn't followed procedure. He even suggested that I had tried to get the family to beat Ian up!

I did get a letter from the regional director and the decision to transfer me was reversed. But nothing happened to Ian. One evening when I was about to go home, Ian got into the lift with me and stopped it mid-floor. I was terrified. He just slapped my face really hard. Then he grabbed me by the throat and began to squeeze. I could see the hate on his face. 'You need to leave here or one day you'll have a nasty accident. Got it, bitch?'

I don't work there any more. Ian still does."

03

SUZI, WAITRESS
HOUSTON, TEXAS, U.S.

> A wretched soul, bruised with adversity.
> We bid be quiet when we hear it cry,
> But were we burdened with like weight of pain,
> As much or more we should ourselves complain.
>
> *The Comedy of Errors*, Act II, Scene 1

"How you doin'? Right... OK... So... Suzi. Hi. OK, so I don't want anyone else to go through what I've had to go through.

Well, hey, I was a victim of domestic violence... I was married last spring, but within three months my husband was physically and emotionally abusive. I left him, but the threats only escalated. From there it went from, 'I want to kill you' to 'I'm gonna kill you,' and some more graphic details which I can't repeat to you.

The County Sheriff's Office put out a warrant for my husband's arrest on October 8th. The next day, I went into work as usual at the restaurant in the mall. I told a co-worker what was happening at home. That co-worker then got security involved. The security guard came over to talk to me and said, 'OK, we need to talk to the store manager.'

Initially, the manager promised me that the restaurant would come up with a safety plan, in case my husband showed up. But later—just hours into that same shift—the story changed big time. The store manager comes up to me and says, 'You need to leave the restaurant.'

I said, 'What do you mean I need to leave?'

She's like, 'Honey, you need to leave right away.'

I'm like, 'Why? What's going on?'

She said, 'Well, you need to leave. Just told ya. You're a threat to the store. You're putting yourself in danger and you're going to put others in danger by being here. You need to go. Now, y'hear?'

I was told that, unless I could provide a police report or an order of protection, I couldn't continue to work there. But I found out the same day that an order of protection wouldn't come into effect until my husband was served with another order by the police—and, anyways, he would have to be on the run. Since I couldn't provide a protection order, I had to leave the restaurant.

My manager said, 'Well, you know, you put yourself in this predicament, honey. And, anyway, I have enough to do without your problems as well. Good luck darlin'.' She added, 'This is your own fault, sweetie. You did this to yourself.'

Walking out of the store crying was a tough call. Everybody staring and nobody caring. And some laughing.

Domestic violence is something that affects—they reckon—one in four women in the United States. I think that employers should say not 'what if' this happens in their place of work, but 'when'. I know now that my employer was obliged to make reasonable accommodations to allow me to keep doing my job. My manager told me not to come back for several days. 'What you're doing to me,' I said to her, 'is making me feel like even more of a victim.'

I was paid basic money for that time off, but I just wanted to be working. I needed the money real bad. I was eventually put back on the schedule after speaking with my manager's boss a number of times, but that didn't work because my manager just put every obstacle she could in my way. And on two occasions she humiliated me in front of the public by talking about my husband and his relationship—or non-relationship—with me. She also suggested that I was a prostitute.

I've decided to take my case to the State Attorney General's Office. I don't want anybody else to have to go through this. It's hard enough to be a domestic violence victim. Dealing with the threats. Wondering. But you have to be strong, don'tchya?

Well now, my husband caught me going home one night, asked me for money and beat me up. The next week someone else beat me up, too. Couldn't see her face. I know it was a woman. I was in hospital for two weeks."

04

LORNA, OFFICE ADMINISTRATOR
DUBLIN, IRELAND

> In time we hate that which we often fear
>
> *Antony and Cleopatra*, Act I, Scene 3

"My name is Lorna. Hello, how are you? OK, well, I live at home with my mother. In Dublin.

I applied for my first full-time job with a large and prestigious organization. No, I can't mention its name. I was interviewed by my would-be boss. The interview was very pleasant and brief. To my delight and total surprise, I was offered the job, even though I had no real experience.

I began work and shared a large office with my boss, Susan. We got on extremely well and she went out of her way to help me and I quickly learned the skills of an office administrator. She appeared to be happy with my performance and was full of praise for my achievements. I loved working there and had never been happier in my life. Everything was just... really good fun, and I enjoyed the people and the work. The company organized a charity event involving walking on hot stones. I was the first to do it and the CEO was the second.

My boss took extended leave and I did both my own job and hers. The work was intense, but I was delighted to do it. Susan organized a significant monetary bonus for my efforts when she returned, and I was really humbled by her generosity. My mum was delighted that I was so happy.

After a year, Susan hired another girl to work in the office with me. This girl, Sarah, was really nice. However, pretty quickly I began to notice a difference in my boss's attitude. She took work away from me and gave it to the new girl, Sarah. She praised Sarah enthusiastically and said things like, 'It's so nice to have someone intelligent in the office for a change.' I didn't understand and couldn't explain the change in my boss's attitude. I felt guilty and assumed that I had let her down in some way. Pretty soon Sarah didn't talk to me very much. And then not at all.

I had never taken any sick leave and I always did my work on time and correctly. I got on well with everybody in the building and could think of nothing that I had done wrong to annoy my boss.

Gradually, I began to notice changes. For example, I would be asked to look after reception when meetings were held, so I always missed those meetings. That had never happened before. Before, I always attended the meetings. Now, the new girl, Sarah, did. And I would open and sort out the post and bring it to Susan but she would say nothing, where previously we would've discussed items in the post over a cup of tea. To compensate, I started arriving earlier at work and tried to be overly helpful to my boss, but that had no effect. The snide comments from Susan got worse. On one occasion, I asked her for advice on how to deal with a particular customer and she responded: 'How come someone like you who is so clever and manipulative can't deal with customers?'

Sorry. No, it's fine... Hang on a minute while I find a tissue.

Well, it all got worse and worse. My boss would show me how to do something and I'd do it exactly as instructed and then she would say again and again that I'd done it the wrong way. She began shouting at me, sometimes in front of other people. She called me names, some really disgusting. Often in front of people. And what was worse still, she would tell others in the office that I was useless. I asked her several times what I'd done wrong and she would say something like, 'It would just take too long to tell you,' and then she would walk away or pick up the phone or talk to Sarah and ignore me.

I talked to my ma about it because she could see that I was troubled. She said that it was all probably nothing and that it would blow over soon. I decided to gain a qualification because I had attended no courses since leaving school. In my own time, I did an advanced computer course and was the first person in my organization to achieve that qualification. A director of the company heard about this and sent me a note of congratulations. But my boss was silent.

My work continued to decline in volume, until I could do the entire day's work in an hour. I asked for more to do, but always received a comment about not being trusted to do the simplest of things properly. Sarah got all the stuff I'd been doing. I thought I might get fired because I wasn't necessary. And I was bored, so I brought a business book to read at work, until Susan criticized me for wasting the firm's time and money. She took away the book, tore some pages out and threw it away. Eventually, I went to HR and sought help. I was really nervous and thought I'd get into big trouble for complaining. HR listened and explained that it was simply a personality conflict and that I needed to sort it out myself. They said that HR had no role to play. I tried to speak to my boss again but she cut me off saying, 'You're pathetic and just neurotic. Go away.'

Work life continued to be really uncomfortable. I led a quiet existence with my elderly mother and never went out at weekends. Every Monday morning Susan asked me what I had done at the weekend and I always replied, 'Nothing much'. She would just smirk, wink at Sarah and say something like, 'sad' or 'pathetic'. Sarah smirked back. I decided to join an amateur dramatic society and I began to have a social life at weekends. One weekend, I received three offers from men to go on dates! When Susan asked me what I did at the weekend then, I told her about the three offers of dates. She never asked me about my weekends again.

I became pregnant. Stupid. From the moment that I told my boss about my pregnancy, she hassled me and, once, she opened a filing cabinet suddenly so that it hit me hard in the stomach. She did that a few times. After three months, I had a miscarriage. When I received medical advice that I could return to work, I rang Susan to let her know. She said, 'It's nothing to do with me and I couldn't care less what you do,' and put the phone down. Soon after I returned to work, another girl gave birth to a baby girl. I heard that she was coming in to show her baby to her colleagues. I didn't feel up to meeting the happy mother and baby and made it my business to find something to do at the other end of the building. My boss searched the building until she found me and told me that I'd been chosen to make a presentation of a bunch of flowers to the new mother. I was really upset, but did as I was told.

A month or so later, Susan hired a new guy, Ben, to join the office and to work with Sarah. Very soon, and behind Sarah's back, Susan was scathing about Sarah and her work. She then started to make snide remarks to Sarah's face and at one point I saw her spit at her. Sarah went on sick leave. After some time, Sarah was sent to the company doctor who told her to return to work. But her family doctor refused to allow her to return to work. Sarah resigned and rumour had it that she was suffering from severe depression.

I was really at low ebb. I went to work one Monday and felt unwell. Again I went to the HR manager. He listened to my story, but he still felt that it was a personality conflict and could be sorted out by both parties. While he was speaking I suddenly jumped up from my seat, looked desperately around the office and then vomited into his wastepaper bin! I apologized profusely. The HR manager advised me to speak to Susan again and I had a feeling then that they both had discussed me. Well, I don't know, but something snapped and I said to the HR guy, 'Look I'm not as well educated as you, but I do know when wrong is wrong. If you won't resolve this situation immediately, I'm going to go to the CEO and make a complaint. If he won't see me, I'll write to each member of the Board.' The HR manager looked very concerned and told me that he would see what he could do.

The following morning I arrived at work to learn that my boss and I were being moved out of our office and into the open plan area with the rest of the staff on that floor. What infuriated Susan was that photocopiers, servers and other pieces of technology were being moved into our old office. I was beside myself with joy. I had always wanted to be out of the poisonous atmosphere of that small office and felt that I would be safer from my boss in the open plan area. My friends in the open plan welcomed me and helped me to set up my desk. I smiled for the first time in months and, when my boss glared at me, I couldn't remove the smile from my face. And didn't.

Two weeks later, the other girl, Sarah, committed suicide."

05

OSCAR, CALL CENTRE OPERATOR
SINGAPORE

> Now let it work. Mischief, thou art afoot.
> Take thou what course thou wilt!
>
> *Julius Caesar*, Act II, Scene 2

"Hello. I've never done something like this. Are you going to ask questions? Oh, I see. Well, where to start? Where? Well, actually it's hard...

OK, so Sabari was the manager of a small call centre employing around 30 staff, half of whom were either temporary or casual employees. The centre operated in normal office hours with some shifts going on to the early hours of the morning. Sabari was very pleased with the call rate the centre was able to record and believed that his personally monitoring calls on a regular basis kept all staff on their toes. His bosses were pleased too, particularly with the money they made! They became very wealthy.

You know, this man Sabari also appeared to take great pleasure in publicly abusing staff members whom he did not believe met the centre's standards in relation to call rates and customer satisfaction. This wasn't just bullying. This was nasty and physical. He did it for fun and also because he could get away with it. Who was going to stop him? And he also tended to target the temporary and casual staff more than the permanent staff. This behaviour had been going on for some time, sufficient to cause several staff members to seek medical treatment for depression, anxiety and, in two cases, physical wounds. One other thing, he would always say that we were paid only in the pursuit of the centre's objectives. Talking to a neighbour for 'mere idle chatter' was a waste of money—and forbidden, he would tell us. There was also really nothing worse than getting the unpleasant, hard, very painful tap on the head followed by a rebuke of 'Get back on the phone'.

I had been at the call centre for about three months and decided to confront Sabari with the complaints concerning his behaviour; or, if that didn't work, then I was going to raise the issue with senior management. I didn't think much would change, though. I knew that what I was going to do was risky, not least for me! Some staff were initially reluctant for me to take this course of action, as they were fearful of the consequences—the casual staff in particular. But I was determined. I saw Sabari and warned him that I would report him if he didn't stop his ways and particularly if he didn't stop hurting people, either physically or by humiliating them. Maybe I shouldn't have done that. I'd only been there a short time. He listened but said nothing.

Early after lunch, on a Thursday I think it was, Sabari came out of his office and in his usual loud voice started to abuse my colleague and friend Irene for alleged poor information given to clients. Irene ignored his behaviour and started to tap a pencil very loudly on the edge of her desk. This was the signal for all staff to begin tapping pencils on the edge of their desks.

Sabari was immediately taken aback and confused and stopped being horrible to Irene. He said to her, 'What's going on?' She ignored him. He turned on his heel and went back to his office. The staff then stopped tapping.

The next day, Sabari again started to abuse another staff member. He was going to strike her. The response was the same. However, this time he asked no questions and went back to his office, slamming the door.

The following Monday I met Sabari and told him straight out that the call centre staff would no longer tolerate his abusive behaviour and that what had happened on Thursday and Friday the previous week was only the beginning of the action they planned to take, unless he was prepared to behave normally and courteously. Sabari agreed, but then hid the office drinks and coffee and tea supplies. He accused two staff members of theft, hit one of them hard in the face and fired them both on the spot. I think that the police are involved in that incident now.

Two days later, Irene was found very badly beaten up near to the office. The police have no idea who committed the crime. Nothing was stolen."

06

JESSIE, ATTORNEY
AUSTIN, TEXAS, U.S.

> The first thing we do,
> let's kill all the lawyers.
>
> *Henry VI Part 2,* Act IV, Scene 2

"Over here? I have some notes. Oh... I see, here's better? OK.

I had just spent three years in law school preparing for the one and only thing I wanted to do, which was to be a prosecutor. I had joined mock trial teams, taken all the criminal law classes and even had actual courtroom experience as an intern at a major city's district attorney's office. I was, by all accounts, the perfect candidate.

While I had hoped to stay in the DA's office where I had interned, a new election resulted in turnover and my supervisors were gone, so I expanded my search to include other counties in or near major cities where I had attended law school. After passing the bar in November, I got an interview with a prosecutor's office in a suburb of Austin. I was well aware of the conservative reputation of that county and dressed appropriately for the interview. My trial experience and dedication to the job won them over and I was offered a job to start after the Christmas holidays.

I wasn't sure what to expect of the job, but I knew I would have to hide the fact that I was politically a liberal and an atheist due to the nature of politics in the county. Religion and politics are supposed to be off-limit topics at work anyway, right? Besides, I was more apt to talk about a movie I'd seen recently than politics or religion, no matter where I was. I knew, regardless of everyone's differences, we were all working towards the same goal. At least, that's what I thought.

Well, as this was my first real job, I was quiet and obedient, keeping my head down and trying to learn the ropes from the people who had been there for a while. I picked everything up quickly and started off on the right foot, winning my first trial. For some jobs this would have been an 'in' to the team, but the more I did, the more distant my colleagues became. Whenever I walked into one of their offices, the group inside would stop talking and look at me in a way that suggested I'd been the topic of conversation. I felt alienated, but I still tried to fit in.

About halfway through the year, things started to get bad. I was actively made fun of for attempting to be entertaining or trying to enter a conversation. Religion and politics were always topics of conversation at lunch and I guess my silence gave me away. To make matters worse, it was an election year, so talk of politics was all around. I didn't feel comfortable enough to put my Obama sticker on my car because I didn't want people at work seeing it—not that it would have mattered at this point.

There was one guy in particular, a veteran from the Iraq war, who believed he was untouchable. Back then there were big employment laws regarding veterans who took time off for deployment. Anyways, this guy absolutely hated me. I generally deferred to anyone who had been there longer than I had when it came to instructions or rules but, for some reason, nothing I did was ever, ever good enough for him. He berated me on a daily basis. I was belittled in front of others and even in open court. My only ally, an older judge, had to kick this guy out of the courtroom twice for his tirades against me for tiny mistakes I'd made in paperwork. The guy jostled me and followed me to the washrooms, then waited outside and followed me back to my office. He didn't do anything really physical big-time, but it was very intimidating.

My co-workers didn't stick up for me either. They told me that was just how he was and that I should suck it up and deal with it. I began to wake up every morning feeling sick, terrified of what he might do that day. Sometimes he blamed me for a mistake that was later discovered to be his own. Other times he'd misplaced some papers and accused me of stealing them. There was never an apology. He screamed and screamed at me in front of a police witness I had been talking to… The final straw was being called to his office and standing in the doorway as he cursed at the top of his lungs, ending with him throwing a large stapler which hit a wall inches from my head. When it missed he threw a heavy law book at me—and that hit me square in the face.

As I had done on multiple previous occasions, I locked myself in my office and just wept. In an office where open doors were the norm, mine was constantly closed for the last three months of my employ. I called my parents almost daily, begging them to let me move in with them at their new home in Missouri, but they just thought I was being silly. I gained weight, had my shrink up my antidepressants and basically went straight to bed when I got home at 6pm.

The lawyer in me still had a grasp on reality and I began keeping a log of things he did to me—date, time, location, witnesses. After four months the log was 17 pages long. I wrote up a resignation letter and included this calendar of abuse, stating that because of this treatment, I was leaving. So I resigned. When I left that last time, I was not wished well by anyone and the Iraq vet and one of the partners just laughed as I got in my car. A week later, I received an email from the veteran who wrote that I was a fat bitch, a terrible prosecutor, a liberal and that I should get out of law.

The next three years were tumultuous to say the least. I tried prosecuting for a different office, but my self-esteem had been knocked so low that I was basically asking to be taken advantage of. I decided to quit law. I was finally accepted into a Master's course in marketing, from which I will graduate this coming May.

The effects of that terrible job have been long-lasting. I began having panic attacks about completely random situations and isolating myself from people for days at a time. My medication was changed multiple times. All no good. Finally, after a complete breakdown in my apartment one afternoon, I called my doctor and got the first available appointment. He didn't know more than my medical history showed—I had a therapist who talked to me about my problems. Once I had told him about the last three years, my panic attacks, my fear of leaving my apartment or interacting with anyone and my general anxiety about re-entering the workforce, he diagnosed me with severe depression. Now, with a different combination of medication and bi-weekly therapy, I'm working towards recovery.

My panic attacks have lessened significantly, but I still suffer from recurring dreams and certain triggers in daily life. I lost three years and the potential for a strong career in law. I have not set foot in the state of Texas in that time and I have many friends I want to visit, but the anxiety is too great.

I'm rebuilding my life and will begin a new career in May. I should be excited about a new opportunity, but instead I'm very nervous and hesitant… I'm sorry? Pardon me? Oh, my limp? Yes, he did that too."

07

MATT, ENTREPRENEUR

SÃO PAULO, BRAZIL

> And thus I clothe my naked villainy
> With odd old ends stol'n out of holy writ,
> And seem a saint, when most I play the devil.
>
> *Richard III*, Act I, Scene 3

"Hurting people, in any way you may wish to consider, has always been something that I enjoy. As a child, as a teenager and as an adult, I enjoyed the process of hurting, of humiliating people, of hurting people physically and getting away with it. Sure I did. Still do. If someone crossed me, I would get my revenge—maybe not immediately but at some point—and the punishment would be severe, in some cases fatal. Well, sure. It happens. Go figure.

Say, are you cold? The air con's really good. Sure? Well, say if you are. More coffee? OK, well, I loved wealth and had no compunction whatsoever about getting and keeping money that I had genuinely or dishonestly earned. As with hurting people, I was also very good at keeping money.

I was born in Mumbai to American parents. They happened to be in Mumbai because my father was a successful importer of spices. I had an older brother, Max, whom I detested from the outset and a younger sister, Jennifer, whom I adored. The family was well off and enjoyed all the finer things of life. After toing and froing between Mumbai and New York with some occasional stops in Beijing, Singapore and London, we moved to New York permanently, during which time my father lost his business (cash flow and some major stupidity) and then his life. Threw himself off the Brooklyn Bridge. Idiot.

My mother discovered quickly that she was penniless and had to take a job in a Manhattan store. She lived with us children on the Lower East Side, not a cheap option in the 1940s, but still cheaper than elsewhere. We were in a one-bedroomed apartment and that made sleeping arrangements difficult, but at least my mother kept the family together, and she put food on the table as the saying goes. She wanted me to have some kind of academic training, but knew that costs would be prohibitive. In any case, I wasn't particularly adept at high school, unlike my brother and sister. My accomplishments were in other directions. I was a tall, strong boy and I easily made sure other kids gave me money—small amounts so that the 'pain' was low-key and because then the likelihood of teachers and parents becoming involved was… minimal. I was sly, yes, and would pretend to befriend a boy in order to gain trust and money. Only rarely did I have to resort to any violence but, when I did, the punishment was hard and harsh. Not once between the ages of 9 and 17 did I get into any trouble for violence or theft.

On my 17th birthday, my mother went out ostensibly to work that morning, and simply never returned. My siblings and I had no idea if she had died or had simply run away. Whatever, I never saw her again... We had no other relatives as far as we were aware. My elder brother promptly enlisted in the US Navy and my sister enrolled to train as a teacher, paying for her studies by washing dishes and tutoring small kids in mathematics. I decided to stay in New York and live with my friend Stevie Medoza. Steve wasn't wealthy, but had a good job with a Manhattan advertising agency as a runner or something. He was smart and eventually wanted to become a copywriter. I stole small amounts from Steve and, whether he knew it or not, he never said anything and was always generous and helpful to me.

One day, Stevie was unwell, and I went to the ad agency to explain Stevie's indisposition but also offered myself up for work. When I went home that evening, I packed my few things into a suitcase and left the apartment without saying anything to Stevie. I found a room in a boarding house. It was horrible and it stank, had cockroaches, but was very cheap. The next day I went back to the ad agency, told some stuff about Stevie and his honesty as well as his illness being long-term, and was made a full-time member of the agency staff. I never saw Stevie again. I couldn't care less.

Well, I went from strength to strength at the ad agency, keeping my nose clean, but treading on others' shoulders and heads and eventually becoming an account manager and then an account director for three huge pieces of business—one in automotive, another in government bonds and the third in retail. I had several secretaries and PAs—all mostly useless. I slept with most of 'em. One I remember was looking smug sitting on the settee in my office and I had to hit her... You kidding? Of course there was no trouble.

You read *The Prince*? Niccolo Machiavelli. Cunning and duplicity. In it he says, 'Everyone sees what you appear to be, few experience what you really are.' I like that. And *The Art of War* by Sun Tzu? He says, 'Appear weak when you are strong and strong when you are weak.' I love that!

Well, colleagues hated me, but management loved me. I made a great deal of money for the firm and got very close to my clients at senior executive levels. I broke rules and made money. I knew, for instance, that a car manufacturer was about to buy out a competitor—a loose tongue over a drunken dinner. You know the secret is to drink water, not vodka? Course you do. Anyway, shazzam, I bought stock through an offshore company and made a fortune. Similarly I did the same many times with information that I shouldn't have had or shouldn't have acted upon.

So, eventually I left the ad agency and went to another as deputy CEO. And I took my clients with me. I made sure that the CEO received no credit for anything and any losses at the agency I made sure stuck to him. After a time they let him go and I was invited to join the Board, after which I fed information to another agency and those guys very soon made a successful takeover bid. I made a lot of money and became CEO of the takeover agency.

Look, I have another appointment in a moment, so let's wrap this up. I've been accused of many things and I've had close calls, but I know how to deflect trouble and I also know what presses people's buttons—what makes them emotional or angry—and if you can do that so that the man or woman shows their 'wrong' side in public, why, you're more than halfway there. Easy. One time, I turned a big-time accusation round and sued the agency and won a multimillion-dollar out-of-court settlement. Seven million, actually. And then I left and set up a consultancy to develop conferences similar to the World Economic Forum at Davos. I set up just two before I stopped. You have to know when to stop. Each one promised delegates contact with the world's greatest business heads and politicians, and each one promised the business heads and leaders contact with each other and top influencers. The income from delegates and sponsors was huge and I had all kinds of backhanders. Y'know—to arrange this and arrange that—all done at a distance of course. The organization fronting this never mentioned my name, of course, and there was zero connection with me. Yeah, I'm comfortable. Look around. What do you think? Happy? Sure, I'm happy. What's not to be happy about?"

08

JEFF, RESTAURANT WORKER
VANCOUVER, BRITISH COLUMBIA, CANADA

> O villain, villain, smiling, damned villain.
>
> *Hamlet*, Act I, Scene 5

"I was a high school student who made good grades and was never, ever in trouble. To save money for college, I worked part-time at a local fast food restaurant owned by, let's call him, Mr. Smith. After the manager quit and walked off the job, Mr. Smith needed to fill the position immediately, so he hired Dave without doing a background check. A couple of employees knew Dave had a criminal record, with several convictions for violent crimes. They had a meeting with Mr. Smith and told him that they feared for their safety if Dave was hired. Mr. Smith thought that they were overreacting, dismissed their claims and hired Dave anyway. He said that Dave was just right to sort things out.

Within a week, several co-workers observed Dave making physical threats to me. He always smiled horribly, had terrible teeth and awful breath. The stuff of nightmares. I told Mr. Smith about those threats and that I feared for my safety. He took no action and actually laughed in my face and later, I learned, behind my back. He encouraged others to make fun of me, to tease me and on two occasions his thugs deliberately splashed hot oil over me—something that would normally have been met with instant dismissal. Three days later while I was emptying the trash, Dave attacked me. I sustained a concussion, a fractured left clavicle and soft tissue injuries to my face.

I filed a workers' compensation claim. After seeking legal advice, my parents also filed a third-party civil lawsuit, alleging that, but for Mr. Smith's gross negligence and wanton disregard for my safety, I wouldn't have been seriously injured. Mr. Smith's lawyers tried to assert that I was limited to workers' compensation benefits only and asked the court to dismiss my lawsuit. The attorneys claimed that their client might have been negligent in hiring Dave, but that Mr. Smith's actions did not constitute gross negligence or a wanton disregard for my safety. The court disagreed and awarded me $120,000 in damages for my medical bills, expenses, lost wages and an amount for my pain and suffering.

Dave still works for Mr. Smith. I don't. I haven't worked anywhere for a year. And I haven't yet received a red cent of what's due to me."

09

CHEN, ENGINEER
BEIJING, CHINA

> For honesty coupled to beauty is to have honey a sauce to sugar.
>
> *As You Like It*, Act III, Scene 3

"Excuse my English, please. Here's my situation. I was in the break room with other workers and we were talking about a job we had to do in the factory. I had said very little. There was one man who likes to tell people what to do, even though he is not a manager. He takes money from people by threatening them and steals from the factory. Everybody's frightened. We've all seen him do it. In the break room this man made a nasty comment about me and I told him to relax, just relax. He took the spoon from the sugar dish and threw sugar at me. I was shocked and shook it off. I felt myself getting angry, but I just told him to calm down, but he started swearing at me and calling me terrible names. He insulted my family.

There were other people in the break room and one went to tell a manager that we were fighting. The manager thought that she meant we were physically fighting, which we weren't. We were having an argument—but my co-worker was shouting and swearing and I was just trying to get him to calm down. To be honest, I was frightened. He kept saying that he would cut my throat.

When the manager showed up, he told us to explain what was going on. I started to tell my side of the story, but then my co-worker threw the big sugar dish at me! It hit me in the chest and the sugar sprayed in my face and eyes, as well as over the rest of me. It hurt and I immediately tried to get the sugar out of my eyes. The manager did what he could to try to settle my co-worker down, but it didn't really work, so someone called the police. I wanted to protect myself. I made certain that the manager told the police that my co-worker had thrown a sugar bowl at me and that he and other employees had seen it happen.

The co-worker was sent home on suspension and I stayed to finish the day. I didn't really talk to anyone about it because I didn't take any other breaks that day. I just wanted to get my work done and go home. The next day, I came in to find out that I had been suspended and that there would be an investigation. Apparently, no two stories were exactly the same among the witnesses, so both me and the other man were fired after five days of suspension.

I haven't got another job. The man has threatened me and he has powerful friends. I'm scared because I know what these people can do. He knows where I live, I think. No, I know he does… and I know he follows me."

10

DEAN, LATHE OPERATOR
BIRMINGHAM, UK

> One pain is lessened
> by another's anguish.
>
> *Romeo and Juliet,* Act I, Scene 2

"My name is Dean. Hi. Here's fine, thanks.

Well, the firm where I work produces tools for the motor trade. About 18 months ago I was working on my lathe, minding my own business. I looked up because someone called my name and the next thing I knew, a heavy piece of wood smacked into my temple. I'm big, as you can see—and strong, but I fell over and all I could hear was my supervisor laughing. Billy's his name. He was laughing so loud and then his mates were, too. I felt dazed from the incident and couldn't see straight, but I pretended to keep working. Later, I was sick.

Billy regularly fired a nail gun at staff and pretended to fire it at close range, without saying it was empty. That was terrifying. Very soon after the first incident, I had my thumb and my left wrist broken in a machine, two weeks after I had warned Billy that it was dangerous. And I had my pay docked after taking a mate to hospital who had shot himself in the leg with a nail gun. Or so they said. Everyone knew it was Billy. And the bastard would throw wood or small pieces of metal at staff nearly every day.

No safety gear or goggles were available, even though they should have been by law. We had to buy our own and very often, if we did, they were stolen. We were forced to pay inflated rates for any safety equipment from the boss, including as much as £8 for a pencil. Pay was regularly docked for taking too long on a job or for cleaning tools. And we were warned not to join a union.

The factory was a revolving door, with staff hired on the spot and fired on the spot, too. I helped train more than 30 people, but most left quickly—often within six months.

This? Yes, well, it does still hurt. That was from a nail gun."

11

MARCIE, BANKER

LONDON, UK

> Friendship is constant in all
> Save in the office and affairs of love.
>
> *Much Ado About Nothing*, Act II, Scene 1

"Hello. Pleased to meet you. Well, it all got quite complicated… I'll do my best. Let's see… Where to begin?

I'd been invited at the last minute to attend a conference. All I knew was that some of the topics were going to be valuable for my role in the bank for which I worked. It was the graveyard slot, just after lunch, and the bankers assembled in the ballroom of the London hotel were sleepy. The woman in the seat next to me—who was to be one of the afternoon's speakers—was surreptitiously sending emails on her iPhone. Bored, I glanced across and saw that the messages going to and fro were composed predominantly of kisses. I positioned my head so that I could see more and realized that the other side of this conversation appeared to be in the room. The text exchange was, as it happens, an unflattering running commentary on the current speaker, leavened with endearments and lascivious thoughts and a plotted assignation once the conference was over. I turned around to see if I could spot the man equally engaged with his phone, but half the audience seemed to be prodding at gadgets in their laps.

The current speaker was coming to a lacklustre close and my neighbour calmly got up, walked to the stage, positioned herself at the lectern and proceeded to give a presentation on the success of diversity policies at her bank. She hadn't been introduced, the previous speaker hadn't been thanked and nobody had a clue as to what was going on. But her presentation was excellent—amazing actually—to the point, balanced and educated. The audience looked up from their mid-afternoon torpor. This woman was good. I looked at the programme and realized that this was to be my new boss at the bank. I'd only met her once before, and then only fleetingly. I'd just been promoted from a different department. I wondered what was going on beneath her quiet, confident behaviour? And who was the man she'd been texting?

Offices are the strangest of places, don't you think? It's perhaps not surprising that all sorts of dysfunctional things start to happen. In the past 15 years at the bank at which I worked, I had become aware that there were two people who were regarded as toxic—really ghastly people who fired anyone who got in their way, who had HR seemingly in their pockets and who got away with some terrible, malignant and malicious things. I have no idea how all that happened or why senior people didn't get involved or do something. Well, one of those people worked in a totally different division from me and I had had no dealings with him, thankfully, but I knew people who had. Stories about what this manager did were shocking—abusive, violent, terrible—but he always seemed careful never to step over a line that would have got him into serious trouble. Well, he's been posted abroad now. Maybe because they needed to get shot of him? I don't know. I didn't know then who the other toxic person was. Then I found out.

I remember when I opened that email from my boss. She'd spent a year making my life miserable in every way imaginable—not accepting work after having chased me for weeks, criticizing me openly and in meetings with very senior people present, making me look stupid in front of clients, the media and colleagues, blaming me for her or the department's mistakes, accusing me of not being a team player... My salary was good, but she'd made sure that any opportunity for further promotion was nil, and she bad-mouthed my name in the industry so I had little room for advancement. My crime? She thought (wrongly) that it was me who'd talked about her affair with a general manager. He was obviously the guy at the conference and, I now know, a 'staging post' up the promotional ladder. Her plan hadn't worked out. The info about the affair had gone viral and people were secretly, and not so secretly, delighted that here was one thing where she hadn't won. The GM had to resign but she'd managed to stay. For that she blamed me—not because she cared one iota for him, but because she'd been stopped in her tracks.

Her emails to me were never one word longer than strictly necessary and the summons on that day never gave any clue as to what she wanted to see me about. I briefly wondered whether it was ominous, but decided it wasn't. When she had bad news to impart she got her PA to ring and make an appointment. Or so I thought. Her office was two floors above my own and occupied the corner of the tower, with a view down towards St Paul's. There was a bound copy of Milton's *Paradise Lost* on her bookshelf next to a myriad of popular business books. She was waiting for me, pacing up and down like a small, irritable animal in a cage.

'Thanks for coming up,' she said, not sounding remotely grateful. 'Did you see that nonsense in the press this morning?'

I nodded.

'Good. We need someone to take the rap for that and I've put it out that it was you who leaked the information. It wasn't. It was me. Upstairs are furious. With you. And grateful to me. Don't worry—the case is watertight, just in case you're wondering. In addition, I've let it be known that you were on the take and we're looking into a count of fraud against you. That may not stick, but people will think certain things about you. They do already.'

'But… that's not true,' I said in disbelief.

'Of course it's not, you idiot,' she replied smoothly. 'But I think you'll find that we'll make it stick… Well, we'll do the best we can, rest assured.' She turned to go back to her desk. 'Stay in touch,' she said."

12

PAMELA, CALL CENTRE SUPERVISOR
SYDNEY, AUSTRALIA

> The common curse of mankind, folly and ignorance, be thine in great revenue!
>
> *Troilus and Cressida*, Act II, Scene 3

"Good afternoon. Happy to help... I have to go in around half an hour. Is that OK?

Well... I would say that visionary companies pursue a cluster of objectives, of which making money is only one—and not necessarily the primary one. Yes, I know that they seek profits, but they're equally guided by a core ideology—and a sense of purpose beyond just making money. Yet paradoxically, the visionary companies make more money than purely profit-driven companies. Look, it's a very interesting point that goes against conventional wisdom—which states that the overwhelming priority of a business should be, first and foremost, to make a profit for its owners; but it's a view that has been gaining some support in the media, I think.

The shareholders who own businesses in the group for which I worked had other, non-financial, priorities in addition to their financial objectives. Not that they didn't want to earn a good return on their investment, but it wasn't their only goal, or even necessarily their main one. They were also interested in being excellent at what they did, creating a great place to work, providing a first-class service to customers, having productive relationships with their suppliers, making useful contributions to the communities in which they lived and worked and finding great ways to lead their lives. All good stuff, I think you'll agree?

It all takes me back to when our senior manager first started and she spoke to each of us individually about her background and philosophy. I'd waited several weeks for my turn, by which time I knew all about her anyway. Perhaps she knew that, since she seemed to be particularly weary when trotting out her biographical details: worked in a high-powered sales job, climbed up the ladder, divorced, company bought out, took redundancy, went travelling, divorced again, wanting a new challenge. At the end of the meeting she announced, 'I'm passionate about customer service!' The cynic in me felt like telling her that she had got the job and that there was no need to still be in interview mode; but a small part of me was hopeful, since I felt that our customer service had hitherto fallen by the wayside—the emphasis simply being on getting through as many calls as possible to maximize profits.

At the beginning there were a few changes, the most significant being that all staff received some fresh customer service training. Awards for 'best customer service' and 'best teamwork' were instituted and there was even talk of the focus on call-times being relaxed. The new call-time charts no longer had gold, silver and bronze medals for volume. Just admonishments for poor-quality service. This, however, was as far as any attempts at improving customer service were made, before the pendulum swung wildly in the other direction.

Generally, my 'I love customer service' manager could be found at her desk facing the three banks of screens our people work on, watching what I assume to be a live feed of our call stats. Very rarely did she leave her post. Occasionally she could be seen typing one of her aggressive memos or 'newsletters', which tended to criticize staff by name for one reason or another, or else to remove yet another small privilege, like being able to visit the water-cooler between breaks. She kept stressing the importance of staying seated without fail for the duration of workers' shifts. She said that every time someone left his or her desk, the company would lose a call. She insisted that people minimize lavatory or water breaks. This, she said, could equate to over 2000 lost calls in a week, with a loss of revenue that the company couldn't afford in this 'difficult economic climate'.

And staff weren't allowed to talk to each other. More calls lost, she reckoned. A colleague had the temerity to ask her once if this was quantity over quality, because we weren't receiving much training and were making mistakes. That person was pilloried and has more or less been demoted and certainly isolated.

And teamwork went out of the window. Here was the person who instituted a 'best teamwork' award telling us explicitly not to help each other out! And she was supposed to be the great champion of customer service. Any ideals of customer service were subordinated to the aim of getting through as many calls as possible to ensure our firm maximized its profits.

Experienced staff were becoming increasingly disgruntled, losing motivation and voting with their feet. If they resigned, she threatened to give lousy references. But, as it takes someone about six months at least to become proficient on all the systems and to begin posting sub-three-minute call times, then she wasn't doing the company or herself any favours. She couldn't have cared less. The company thought she was great.

She invented new rules. No getting up at all for any reason during a shift. No talking to a colleague. No doodling. No outgoing calls to be made, ever. No use of mobile phones, ever. And our phones had to be turned off during working hours. No using the internet. Any breach of any of these rules, she said, would mean instant dismissal. One strike and out.

And she practised what she preached. Listen, there was one operator who was pregnant and she couldn't sit still for so long without visiting the bathroom. Another had recently had a back operation and needed to get up and walk around from time to time. Another was in a wheelchair and needed water regularly. The pregnant woman fainted one day and had to be rushed to hospital. The man with the poor back was readmitted to hospital and the woman in the wheelchair had to leave the business. No, I don't know what happened to her."

13

FRANKLIN, MANAGEMENT CONSULTANT

NEW DELHI, INDIA

> We know what we are,
> but not what we may be.
>
> *Hamlet*, Act IV, Scene 5

"I'll have to tell it my way, I'm afraid. Oh, OK, that's fine then...

Well now, I've lived here for eight years and to begin with it was all terrific. I travelled around the country. Became really interested in the history of the country's different cultures. Then... listen, leadership is all about maintaining a position of power instead of empowering others. You understand? I've always thought that an unhealthy amount of charisma can lead to narcissism. And like the Greek myth of Narcissus, many like him find their fate in tragic death.

This is relevant, I promise. Essentially, the story of Julius Caesar is less about the man who ruled Rome and more about how his arrogant and charismatic personality was the character flaw that led to his untimely death, a civil war in Rome and the beginning of the end of the world's most powerful empire. Caesar, a successful general, assumed a dictatorship over the people. While Rome was still technically a republic, Caesar was the boss. Though the conspirators who plotted his murder didn't approve of his authoritative style, many in Rome loved him for the freedoms and prosperity he brought.

Nonetheless, Caesar's demise was a result of his own arrogance. It is rare that conceit produces consensus in leadership. I think that a problem comes when leaders believe themselves so special that ordinary rules no longer apply. Generalized pride—as opposed to being proud of specific things—is one of the most serious leadership failings, because it can lead to so much else that is wrong. This was certainly the case with Caesar. His victories in the political arena and on the battlefield gave him a pride that led him to believe that he was invincible and even divine. He was neither.

In another Shakespeare play, Macbeth became so obsessed with maintaining his rule that he disregarded all morality. Power-hungry and paranoid, he ended up having anyone killed who threatened his kingdom. Again, it was charisma and pride that led to the fall of a once great leader. This is exactly the case with my CEO, the only difference being that he didn't kill his predecessor, but just made sure that the predecessor took the whole blame for making huge losses. Our new CEO trusted nobody and would get rid of anyone, absolutely anyone, who got in his way. He took advantage of others due to his position, for example, by delegating ridiculous amounts of work to people and then passing off the work as his own. Ditto any achievements and successes. Often this kind of situation involved psychotic behaviour and, on one occasion, the finance director was locked in a cupboard for three hours. That's absolutely true. And the guy's secretary had orange juice thrown over her during a board meeting. Once, he slapped another secretary for smiling during a meeting and he touched another member of senior staff where he shouldn't have, on several occasions. All to humiliate. Secretaries tried to complain. But nothing ever happened.

In public meetings he was cool, smooth, polite and always seemed to listen to everyone's point of view. He spoke calmly, even when the air-conditioning was off. After meetings, though, with one or possibly two people in his office, he would rant and rage, often threatening all sorts of terrible things. He fired someone for getting the wrong biscuits for a meeting once (he only allowed Nimkin or Milk Shakti) and, on another occasion, fired someone who hadn't heard something he'd said. The fellow he fired had a well-known hearing problem. Yes. The CEO was always very clever at proving that someone was not capable of performing their role, or of claiming that they were simply out of their depth. He would do these things under the pretence of caring—and people fell for it.

Where is he now? He's still CEO. Me? I got fired. For taking a day off sick when he wanted me in a meeting. I don't have a new job yet."

14

DAVID, CORPORATE COMMUNICATIONS MANAGER
MANILA, PHILIPPINES

> There is no darkness but ignorance.
>
> *Twelfth Night*, Act IV, Scene 2

"Hi. The best way I can tell you this story is to read an excerpt of the transcript of a conference call that had 1,000 employees on the same call. The call was led by my ex-CEO, who at the time was in our Manila office near Bonifacio Global City. This is more or less what he said. I have the transcript:

'There are a couple of things I want you all to realize and really get sunk in. Be of zero doubt. Zero. If it doesn't sink in and you don't believe what I'm about to say, then this isn't going to work. Is that clear? I hope it is. I really hope it is. OK? If you don't buy what I'm saying, then I'm going to ask you to leave the company. Yep, just go. And I don't mean that in a bad way; I mean that we have to get the new products into a place where they're going to be successful and I'm here to tell you that they're going to be successful for a long time. They'll only be successful if you make it so.

If you don't, you've failed and you can leave. If you think that you're going to fail, then please leave right now. Kay?

'I will take full credit for what works and full accountability for anything that's not right. You can blame me for it. I was here near the beginning of this business and I'm proud of what I've done. I don't care what the press says. I don't care if people leak information. I take full responsibility. I also want to clear up the fact that leaking information or anything around these products isn't going to bother me. It doesn't bother me. I'm not changing direction. When you hear about what we're doing, it's very serious stuff and it's very forward-thinking, and nothing that you do, or that anyone out there does, is going to change that direction.

'Next thing is, if you don't use the products yourselves and you're not invested 100 percent in the success of the business, you owe it to everybody else in the enterprise to leave. I want these things used. It goes with the job. If you think what's going on right now is a joke and you want to joke about it, you should get your stuff up and leave today. I'm not kidding. Our software is the best in the world. I'm going to be very specific about this… excuse me a minute…

'Hey, David, put that camera down right now. Dave, you didn't hear me. Put the camera down. Get out. Put. That. Camera. Down… You're fired. ******g out! ***k off. Out now!

'OK... That was a ******g idiot who now doesn't work here. Kay? If you guys think that the board and I have not been committed and won't stay committed, you're wrong…

The company has spent hundreds of millions on this... The board of directors is committed, I'm committed....'

Well... my name is David and I was in the communications department. I was a corporate comms guy and was with the CEO during this call—and had been asked specifically by him to take photographs for the company's intranet. Good, huh?"

15

MARIA, AUTOMOTIVE FITTER
MEXICO CITY, MEXICO

> There is thy gold,
> worse poison to men's souls,
> Doing more murder in this loathsome world.
>
> *Romeo and Juliet*, Act V, Scene 1

"Hello. I've come with my friend Maria because she can't explain what happened very well. Is that OK? *Sentar aquí María. El hombre va a hablar y voy a hablar. ¿OKAY?* Sit here Maria. The man will talk and I will talk. OK? Nobody will say anything bad. Yes? *Nadie va a decir nada malo. Si?* Ah no, but maybe some water. Thank you...

Last year, when she worked for a company in Germany, she told her boss that she suffered post-traumatic stress disorder and depression after a big illness that her husband had suffered. But her boss subjected her to an 18-month ordeal of pain. What type of thing? He recorded her voice and played it back to her in front of other staff, laughing and mimicking her accent. He kept asking her if she was on drugs because she comes from South America, and also because she was on medication.

She worked hard and did her job well. At first, all the staff in her group liked working with her because she was careful and fast. People said that. But not her manager and his gang. He was angry that people liked her more than him. He did all kinds of things. He got his friends to steal the chocolate that she kept in her locker. She had a collection of miniature flags that she brought in to show people, and he stole those too. He got her to pay him money each week. Protection he said. He got one guy to tell her every day to show her footballing skills because she was South American… you know? Pele? Lionel Messi? Diego Maradona? Every time people came into the building he would roll a ball to her—like a party trick at a funfair—and she was supposed to kick it back. To start with it was a joke, but then it wasn't funny anymore.

She had a friend at work, Susana, but she also turned against Maria. She began calling Maria a 'bloody foreigner' or *Blutige Ausländer* in German. *Extranjero sangrienta, si, Maria*. I think she was told to do it, but it made my Maria very sad. Her boss always gave other people bonuses, usually store vouchers, for achievements to which Maria had contributed; but Maria, she received nothing. Nothing. And this was done publicly, if you understand me. *Ella recibió nada*. Her boss told his own boss that Maria was no good. Her boss would deliberately make sure that there were always problems with her work. He shouted at her, told her to stand in a corner, made her wear a hat with 'stupid' written on it. *Blöd* in German.

Maria didn't know what to do. Eventually she went to someone who didn't work for the company, a kind of lawyer for workers, and he wrote to the company. Nothing happened, but the humiliation got worse. Then the lawyer went to see someone at the company and again nothing happened.

By the end of last year, the company had begun an investigation and I think that the man, her boss, has since left, but Maria was in such an emotional state that she was unable to complete even basic tasks, so she had to leave. The result is what you see. *¿Entender?*"

16

STEFAN, COMPUTING SPECIALIST
NAIROBI, KENYA

> Love all, trust a few,
> Do wrong to none.
>
> *All's Well That Ends Well*, Act I, Scene 1

"I went out to Africa around three years ago, yes. Great opportunity. An American company, with outposts everywhere. What, exactly, do I do? I'll tell you. Although my boss has no idea. No, really. I trusted him. I trusted a man who has been working in the company from the beginning, for 15 years. This guy always used to tell me everything straight. Or so I thought.

Let's recap that day. I got to work just after 8am. After my usual 30 minutes of answering emails, I did a quick check of the tech news... and then it was off to my first meeting. It is normally chaired by my boss and it runs for almost two hours. It's always terrible—him speaking for the whole time usually—and it was terrible that day, too. This time I was told to make a presentation on something I knew nothing about. He laughed and got angry. He threw a pen at me. Nothing unusual in that, really. He thinks that's funny.

After that, I spent 30 minutes digesting notes from the meeting into actual tasks for myself and the team. Then I asked someone for help with the parts that I hadn't understood or couldn't do. I also spent some time organizing the information I needed for my own staff meeting.

Lunch. Everyone had heard about the meeting and the pen incident. I was eating with the web applications team that day, but they were eating and I wasn't. My boss had helped himself to my food—the great stuff that I had brought from home. Just took it, didn't ask—and smiled. Dared me to react. This wasn't the first time. His buddies laughed. Then he threw half of it away in front of me.

Then I had to go and do some bug database scrubbing... a daily 30-minute task. There are supposed to be trained people to do stuff like this, not me, but my boss thinks that training is a waste. So it always means me. Then another meeting to go through some software stuff. My boss walked in and listened for a while. Then he said to me in a loud voice, 'So, what is it you actually do here?' Everyone went quiet. One person laughed.

My first reaction to this question was that I wanted to leap over the table, grab my boss by the throat, shake him and yell: 'While you sit around on your fat ass, making my life a misery, I'm the one keeping this business going!' And then squeeze his throat hard. And then a bit more. And then, as his eyes pop, I'd laugh into his stupid face...

My second reaction is to take a deep breath, so I do. I take two. Then another for luck... but one day... one day."

17

REBECCA, MARKETING EXECUTIVE
SAN DIEGO, U.S.

> I do love nothing in the world so well as you—is not that strange?
>
> *Much Ado About Nothing,* Act IV, Scene 1

"I moved to Silicon Valley as an inexperienced, innocent young woman. I'd heard startups were all about 'working hard, partying hard', so when I got hired at an all-male startup, I didn't know what I was getting myself into, but it sounded fun.

This sales automation company claimed to automate the entire sales process. But that mythical unicorn failed to ever materialize or solve any sales problems whatsoever, since it was little more than a scam flimsily disguised as technology. Incredibly enough, the company is still operating, in a slightly different market—despite the never-ending complaints they get.

My boss was the co-founder and CEO. All looks, no brain. And damn, was he obsessed with looks (part of the reason I was hired, but we'll get to that in a minute). He quickly became possessive of me and was desperately trying to make a relationship happen for the better part of a year. He'd frequently make me go on trips with him or make me sit alone with him in his office, and he gave me complete preferential treatment over other employees. Eventually we moved to a bigger office, but he continued the awkward treatment by giving me my own office, letting me leave early, taking me for expensive lunches. Mind you, he referred to any woman over 110 pounds as a 'fat chick' and constantly reminded me: 'Just don't eat. Do you want to be ******g fat and disgusting like her? No, you ******g don't.' He would sometimes touch me inappropriately as well—nothing heavy, just a stroke here and a pat there, but it was horrible and I never knew when he was going to do it. I tried to avoid being near him, but he would sometimes creep up behind me and stand too close and then he'd put his arms around me and touch my breasts.

He would also blow imaginary kisses at me in front of people in the office and sometimes he would blow in my ear. I'm sure everyone thought we were having an affair and I started to feel like such a bad human being, and so awkward going into work, that I hatched my escape (I was financially stuck with this job until I found another). He began blaming me for what was going wrong with the business. The creepiest part of all this is that the entire management team appeared to think this was acceptable behaviour and, as a result, no one dared say anything to me or to support me.

To top off the sexual harassment, the management team openly encouraged drug use and regularly did coke... in the office! Over time, as the company began to fail, screaming matches ensued in the office and drug use ramped up. The sales VP, who was a spectacular idiot with a notable coke addiction, enjoyed calling me the 'marketing chick' and said that I should 'leave the real work to the boys'. My only shield from this mega douche was my boss, the CEO, who regularly asked me to get him Xanax, Adderall and a myriad of other drugs. The CEO was a disbarred financial guy who constantly regaled us with tales of his glory days. 'Oh, the things I saw,' he would start, and then go into a long story about his sexual prowess.

Our CEO even promised the entire company that if we 'worked hard' then we could 'relax and get the coke and yachts ready, because everything's about to get crazy'. That's the kind of thing he said. At most staff meetings involving the whole company, if there had been a problem that week, he would make sure that everyone knew where the fault lay. Me, usually. People must have wondered why I was still there. They must have believed that the boss thought that I was crap at my job but great in the sack. I hated it, but couldn't easily leave.

The most impressive part of this startup was their incredible arrogance. Put to positive use, they probably could have done amazing things. The founding team had absolutely no shame, and I'll hand it to them—they had a legit talent for scamming people. Not only could they out-drink and out-drug anyone under the table, they could also bullshit the best of the best. It was all a bit like *The Wolf of Wall Street*.

When I eventually announced I was leaving under the diplomatic guise of going to grad school, the CEO came into my office and verbally and physically attacked me. He grabbed me by my sweater and hauled me up from my chair, and said that I'd never get another good opportunity like this and that I was getting older so I didn't have much life left in my career. I told him I was going to school, and he retorted that I couldn't (couldn't!) because there were a lot of talented guys out there, people with actual pedigrees... And as a woman, I had a lot going against me. He shouted that I should be a high-class escort and that guys really liked my sort of look. He made a lewd expression and an even ruder one with one of his hands. 'You'd be a good prostitute, I reckon,' he said.

I've learned that they employed another woman—still just one—after I left."

18

DENNIS, SOFTWARE DESIGNER
DUBAI, UAE

> The devil can cite Scripture for his purpose.
>
> *The Merchant of Venice,* Act I, Scene 3

"I'll sit here, if that's OK. You're recording this? Right. I see. No, that's fine. It's just a bit disconcerting. Actually, I have quite a few terrible tales from working at an educational software company a few years ago.

The first thing you must understand about this company is that it was run by the oddest pair of individuals. One was a young, mid-20s, silver-spoon-in-his-mouth business guy, let's call him Rudy. Rudy never actually held down a real job in his entire life. The other was a Russian millionaire, let's call him Andrei, who made his fortune after the Soviet Union collapsed, buying up assembly line factories and getting them to operate at a profit, by questionable means. As you can guess, neither of these people had any idea how software was made or how to run a software company. I'll give them credit though—the business model was sound and the idea could have been a huge hit. Unfortunately, they seemed to do everything they could to undermine the company and its employees. I can go on and on in great detail about all the terrible things that happened there that focused mainly around the two owners, but I'll give you the highlights.

First, let's talk about Rudy. After we secured our first major investment of funds, he got all the employees together to announce the good news. Or so we thought. He brought us all down to the parking lot to show us the brand new BMW M6 he'd bought. Then, without telling any employees, or leaving instructions, he went on a three-week five-star vacation.

We did hire a lot of international people to come in and do text and computing translations for us so our product could be global. Rudy had the habit of telling interns he would pick them up at the airport when their planes arrived in Dubai. He never picked them up. We left interns at the airport stranded overnight on more than one occasion. Even worse, there was an instance of Rudy not completing an intern's visa paperwork. This poor guy packed up his entire life to come here to work for a summer and was sent right back once he landed in Dubai.

Rudy would always quote business gurus at us—you know—John Kotter, James Collins, Joe Stiglitz, Gary Hamel… those kinds of people. He had learned great chunks of their philosophies, which he would cite as proof for anything he had decided to do or anything he insisted we believed. One of his favourites was from Jack Welch: 'Focus on a few key objectives ... I only have three things to do. I have to choose the right people, allocate the right number of dollars and transmit ideas from one division to another with the speed of light. So I'm really in the business of being the gatekeeper and the transmitter of ideas.' Oh my God—how many times did he use that one! And the other one he used all the time, right up close to people, was the Paul Dickson, 'Never try to teach a pig to sing; it wastes your time and it annoys the pig.' Not the best quote to use in Dubai. People laughed at first and some Muslims were insulted, but he was serious and never apologized. He would put quotes in emails and any presentation he made had stuff from the management greats. He claimed that he'd been to Harvard, but we all knew that he hadn't been to any university, anywhere. Ever. Often, all the management babble was just out of context, misquoted or just plain wrong for the business. Once someone said that to him—and I have to tell you that that guy didn't last long! Rumour had it that the guy was in hospital for a week.

Rudy would also over-promise potential customers and flat out lie about the capabilities or functionality of our software in order to make a sale. He would then come back to the office and proclaim that we needed to create a feature in, say, two weeks for a customer. Of course this feature would take months to design and develop. We would then be chastised for our lack of ability to deliver Rudy's vision.

With another round of funding, we moved into a new and bigger office in the Dubai Internet City area and meetings were often held in great hotels like the Jumeirah Emirates

Towers, the Shangri-la and Raffles. The new office had all the bells and whistles, plasma TVs, PlayStations, a football table, an amazing kitchen—you name it. When employees used the facilities during lunch or when taking a small break, Rudy would scream at us to get back to work. He said that the facilities were there to attract investors, not to be used by employees. Then he'd shout something like, 'Did Steve Jobs have these problems? Did he employ morons like you?'

We had an excellent local employee who was going through a rough personal patch in his life. A family member was gravely ill and he would sometimes come in late or go home early to visit this family member in the hospital. I was the software manager at the time, so I gave him permission to go visit. When I was questioned by Rudy where this employee was, I told him of the guy's family issues. Rudy called for the immediate firing of the employee. I had to beg. This guy was great at what he did and we couldn't afford to lose him. But he was still fired.

I have plenty more about Rudy, but let me tell you about Andrei now. Well, Andrei would insist that he could solve any software-related technical issue the development team would ever come across, without any actual knowledge or training. He would hear about issues in our development meetings, go home and Google something, then come in the next day and demand we stop wasting time and implement his solutions. Obviously, they would fail miserably and we would waste so much time trying to convince him otherwise. We were then blamed for his decision—and its failure. And he would lash out and really hit someone. Women, too. A few times he tripped people so that they fell down stairs. If he didn't like a person, he would take bits of equipment from their desks and accuse them of theft. Sometimes someone would find their desktop computer console smashed on the floor and that person would get blamed and have money deducted to pay for it. We all knew it was Andrei. One time someone was talking about soccer and hoped that his team (Italy, it might have been) would beat Russia. The guy came in next day covered in bruises, but he never talked about what had happened.

If a task was estimated by the team to take a developer two weeks to do, Andrei would force two developers to work on the same task—and he would expect it to be done in half the time. If you know anything about software development, this is never, ever, possible. At some point, he had a hook for potential investors in Arabic-speaking countries. He promised them a demo of our software in Arabic in a few days' time. We had no one on staff that spoke or could write fluent technical Arabic. Arabic is also a right-to-left text and our software was never designed to handle such an arrangement. And the layout was going to be hard. Also it was going to be necessary to adapt images and symbols as well as graphics to the customs and practices of the Arabic culture. The Arabic written language contains special writing rules that must be supported by the software you use for preparing your technical documentation. Anyway. We worked late many nights in a row to make it happen, and we did make it happen. He never even did the demo. It was all made up.

Also, for some reason, he made his wife a major player in the company's day-to-day operations. The employees rarely saw her, but she did a lot of personal shopping with our money. She spent tens of thousands of dollars. More, probably. Both Rudy and Andrei would also seldom actually come into the office. If they did, it was from about 11am to 1pm. And they installed web-enabled cameras all over the office to make sure employees came in on time and didn't leave early. People would get chewed out if they went to the bathroom for too long.

The saddest part about the job was that we had so many great people working there, and we all knew it. The idea was solid, the software was coming along but, in the end, people just couldn't take the owners anymore, and left one by one.

The company has gone bust now, leaving loads of debts, and you just can't do that in this part of the world. Most staff were owed months of salaries. Rudy is in the States now, I think, and Andrei is nobody knows where, but his brand-new Beemer and his wife's top-of-the-range Range Rover were found at the airport."

19

LEE, TV PRODUCER
KUALA LUMPUR, MALAYSIA

> There is a tide in the affairs of men,
> Which, taken at the flood, leads on to fortune.
>
> *Julius Caesar*, Act IV, Scene 3

"Hi there. Yes, that's fine... I can do that... Perfect...

Well, I worked for the company from 2011 to 2015. Money ran out in 2014, but I couldn't find another job. So essentially I worked for a bunch of time without much pay. My family helped.

Well, we managed to land a contract that had us working on commercial sites for several television shows and things were starting to look like they might turn around... Then the managing director was arrested in Haiti for trying to traffic kids out of the country after the earthquake. You may remember that one. No, I don't know the details, really, or what he was doing.

I was on paternity leave at the time. Contracts were cancelled. I never went back. They shut it down. So, I did a TV production course, searched for a place to work and got hired by this confectionery company that made stuff for worldwide export. I needed the work. Anything. I was all excited to work for a top company in the area, even though it had nothing to do with my training or experience. I worked there for four months only to show up to work one morning for a scheduled company-wide meeting. When I arrived, there was no company-wide meeting. The upper management then systematically fired 25 percent of the staff in four meeting rooms, one by one. Needless to say, the waiting for your 'meeting' was the worst part. It was really an awful day and never what I expected.

I moved on and got a job with a company that produced videos for online use. It seemed a good idea. Sometimes, people start their own companies because they're impossible to work with. Yeah, some people have great ideas and some people want to make a lot of money, but some people are just stupid and have no clue how to run a business. I worked for an idiot who regularly dismissed people from meetings, just told them to get out. He sent employees out to buy food that he'd immediately throw away because it was the wrong rice or the wrong this or that. He'd threaten to withhold pay and pull all types of power moves. He was sure to remind us that he chose to start this company over accepting a guaranteed, six-figure, VP-level job at a multi-billion dollar company. I guess that meant we owed him? He had favourites who got all kinds of good things—extra time off, bonuses, public accolades. And he had those whom he seemed to loathe and picked on all the time. These people became frightened and would do most things he or his gang wanted to get a quiet life. It wasn't fun to see. Me? I kept a very low profile.

Once the company was out of the red, the angel investor and the other two owners promptly forced the guy out—and most of his sidekicks, but not all. When the crunch came, apparently he chucked his iPhone across the law firm when signing the papers. Then as he left the room, he did what Heather Mills allegedly did after the Paul McCartney divorce, and poured a pitcher of water over McCartney's lawyer's head. Our guy did worse. He poured the water—then hit the lawyer on the head with the pitcher.

The business became a better place for a while. Made lots of money. I got a company loan. Times were good. New people were brought in. But two of the original guy's gang were still there and one was made a senior manager. Now the toxicity is back again with a vengeance..."

20

ADHIRA, STORE MANAGER
MUMBAI, INDIA

> Dream on, dream on,
> of bloody deeds and death.
>
> *Richard III*, Act V, Scene 3

"This story happened in England, but I come from India, and that's where I live now. I was working in England before and I had a good time. Apart from this... It's still hard to talk about it, you understand?

The guy... the man... whose name was Stuart, was having an affair with, I shall call her Ursula Prakesh, when he and his friend Geoff smothered her with chloroform, then buried her in a shallow grave. They got 30 years.

Stuart spent at least a month plotting to kill Ursula—one of his many lovers—to prevent her exposing their two-year affair. She was lovely, beautiful, kind, good at her job—a gentle woman. She worked at a big hardware store in Southampton, where Geoff also worked and Stuart was the overall manager. She was reported missing by family members after failing to return home for a planned holiday, and that led to a major police inquiry.

Post-mortem tests established that Ursula was killed using chloroform, then buried alive... At the start of the murder trial, it transpired that Stuart was trying to manage at least three relationships with women at work—all at the same time. Everyone who knew him thought that he was a fantasist who believed that he could do what he wanted with impunity. We knew that Stuart bullied Ursula, but everyone thought that it was mild. Nobody really knew that he was violent and had strict rules that she had to obey. It became clear that he was threatening her with violence if she didn't sleep with him and basically become his slave in the office. No, I'm telling you that's what it was.

People tried to intervene, but HR wasn't interested and the business was making a lot of money, so who cared? Stuart was very clever and the bosses thought that he was exemplary. They got angry with anyone who tried to 'rock the boat'. Some people were forced to leave for being too free in their views about the management.

Geoff was the tough guy and it came out in court that he was the one who pressed a chloroform-soaked tea towel over Ursula's mouth... I think—and the police think—that Stuart and Geoff had tried to kill Ursula before. It seems that she was about to tell the police and the head bosses at work what had been going on. Those bastards killed a bright, ambitious, hard-working and life-loving woman—a daughter, a sister and an aunt. And my best friend. I keep thinking of her last moments... her final thoughts and fears. I constantly imagine the look in her eyes. It keeps me from sleeping."

21

HASSAN, ACCOUNTANT
NICOSIA, CYPRUS

> He that wants money, means,
> and content is without three good friends.
>
> *As You Like It*, Act III, Scene 2

"I was once a glorified bookkeeper, working my way through college to support my family, before I became a financial controller.

Back in the day of paper ledgers and journals, I worked for a leather-goods manufacturer. They made purses, wallets and pad holders—for regular old paper pads, not iPads! I had become increasingly concerned that, while sales remained stable, the cost of goods sold was rising and negatively affecting the bottom line. I usually reported to the vice president, but something was nagging at me about going to him with this problem. Maybe it was the new Mercedes or the ultra-thin Piguet Jules watch that he had recently bought.

So off I went to the president instead. Maybe I shouldn't have, but I did. After I explained to him the matrix of the income statement and its relation to inventory on the balance sheet, he was completely confused. However, he asked me to keep my analysis to myself.

A week later, I was toasting a salary increase and a three-day family weekend at the beach. At the same time the company's president called me and told me in absolute confidence (I had to sign something) that the vice president was taking some of our company's nearly finished products to a small factory that he had set up. His team (the foreman also worked in collusion) would finish the goods there, and sell them on to various distributors and department stores. The fraud was discovered and the vice president, needless to say, went to jail.

What I learned is that sometimes the first sign of fraud is just a feeling that something is not quite right. Numbers may not totally add up or internal controls may be sloppy. A gut instinct can be very helpful when trying to catch white-collar criminals. But there are certainly red flags to watch out for. You may not believe it, but the vice president believed that he was doing the right thing. Totally. From the 2002 Enron fraud scandal and onwards, one of the most interesting behavioural beliefs held by fraudsters is that they totally think that they are acting in a legitimate manner. I've read that prosecutors say these criminals, even after entering a guilty plea, often take months, or even years, to fully accept their guilt.

Our vice president had spent most of his life viewing himself as a law-abiding citizen. He thought that he was performing acceptable practices within the business—that what he was doing was OK. Committing the crime gave him a thrill, a kick. He was, he thought, untouchable. Nobody would accuse him. Money became the object and nothing else mattered. I don't really know what his issues were—whether it was personal debt, investment loss, sheer greed, family expectations, maybe even an addiction. He seemed to dislike most people, saw them as annoying. I don't think that he knew where reality and fantasy began or ended. He liked dramas and made them into crises—and they were always the fault of someone or something else. He liked that, yes. Even when the game was up, he would say that he was only borrowing money and would pay it back and that nobody got hurt. He thought that he was 'owed something'.

When he was arrested, it was at our offices. On his way out, in handcuffs, he caught my eye, smiled and said, 'I'll be after you first. Don't sleep too tight.'"

22

SAM, COMPUTER ANALYST
SAN FRANCISCO, U.S.

> “I follow him to serve my turn upon him:
> We cannot all be masters, nor all masters
> Cannot be truly follow'd.”
>
> *Othello*, Act I, Scene 1

"I joined the company as an experienced hire and was immediately placed on a project which lasted 18 months.

The project was pretty much laid-back, 40 hours a week, with some weekend work required around important project milestones. Overall the environment was friendly and stable, so I had no issues with the workplace. And it was convenient for where I lived. However, I received an average performance appraisal for my first review and was criticized for not networking enough. Now, I'd nailed my KPIs and deliverables, and I had also helped other teams with theirs (I can program in multiple languages, know database design and can 'speak to the business'). None of this was brought up in my review, though, and essentially I was punished for not being a team player. Not a show-stopper, but really annoying nonetheless.

The second situation was much, much worse. A manager called me when I was getting ready to roll off the project and conducted an impromptu interview with me; then, 10 minutes into the conversation, decided to let me know that two client associates were also on the call. So, essentially he had screwed me even before I realized I was being screwed. The manager lied about the new position, saying it was 'dead right for me', when it had nothing to do with my technical background. After the interview, the manager put a hold on me in the company job and promotion system, so I couldn't search for other projects—I was stuck. I was very reluctant, and only agreed to come out for one week to see if the new position, this 'great new opportunity', was a good fit or not.

I arrived on-site, to discover that they wanted me to learn a whole new programming language, stay there for a few years—and completely derail my career! My manager's tone changed and suddenly he demanded I stay for at least a month now, not a week, 'just to see', he said. I argued with him and then his manager, going all the way up to the partner on the project. I was finally allowed to leave after one week, which I did—and then returned to head office. My manager deliberately tried to bad-mouth me to anyone who'd listen. I'm Jewish and he would make frequent and nasty anti-Semitic remarks, but only rarely within others' hearing.

Finally, I rolled onto another new project, with a new boss who had a major inferiority complex and who was the worst micro-manager I ever encountered. After the first week I had a meeting with her to discuss the fact that I simply could not be micro-managed and that we would both need to be flexible in order to ensure a productive working relationship. Things didn't change and actually became progressively worse. Eventually, I spoke with her manager and explained that the situation was unbearable. At one point during the project this manager called my cell phone 15 times in one day, then somehow found my home number and called about 10 times every evening.

After that I decided to call it quits. But this company is like a cult and I'm finding it very, very hard to leave. And I've been threatened with violence three times—no, nothing I could ever prove. I've been told to 'play the game' by my manager and so I sort of do what I'm told now. I've been advised to complete project tasks ahead of time—'or else'. I used to be a 'get up and go' sort of person. I'm not now. My 'go' has got up and gone."

23

SONNY, MENSWEAR DEPARTMENT MANAGER
MINNEAPOLIS, MINNESOTA, U.S.

> When in disgrace with fortune and men's eyes
> I all alone beweep my outcast state.
>
> Sonnet 29

"I do feel ashamed at telling you this, but as a 54-year-old gay man, you would expect that one might be equipped to deal with the slings and arrows of outrageous fortune. Life deals strange hands, don't you think? When you hear about evil management in the media, it's usually about big entrepreneurs and tough multinationals. Well, I've been working for the last decade or more for a large corporation. Like any employee who shows enthusiasm and skill, I've been promoted through the ranks, based on my hard work.

I used to have a reasonable working relationship with all of my colleagues, except one. This man is my immediate supervisor and he's been my boss for some years now. In that time he has been critical of me, has laughed at me for being gay and has tormented me, sometimes physically. He has got others to taunt me and call me names. Everything I say at work in his hearing he tells me—and anyone nearby—that it's nonsense, and he calls me names that relate to my sexuality. He has said publicly that I chase boys and have AIDS.

He says that everything that goes wrong in the department is my fault and he and the others in the department have made that a regular joke, so that people in other departments attribute any failure to me. I'm too old to find another job, I think, and I'm frightened to ask for a reference. I did once try and speak to HR, but they took little notice and I also once had a meeting with a senior manager, but she kept smiling inappropriately. I don't know how my boss gets away with it, but he does. My car has been defaced several times, once with faeces. I've tried time and again to talk to people at work about this but, even if people listen, nothing changes.

I can't afford to just resign and have no work. Yes, I have felt suicidal, I must admit, on several occasions... I don't have any family now and I sometimes think it'd be the easiest way... and I do think that maybe this is all my doing, all my fault. Maybe I've done the wrong things... upset this person. I go to work fearful and just know that every day, every single day, something will happen that will be painful. I'm terrified that one day they will really hurt me. I've lost a lot of weight and regularly feel really unwell. I have no friends at work and just don't know what to do...."

24

MELANIE, ADVERTISING EXECUTIVE
LONDON, UK

> Smooth runs the water
> where the brook is deep.
>
> *Henry IV Part 2*, Act III, Scene 1

"I worked for a very small company with under 20 employees and we were discussing rebranding the business with the three directors, something that was very exciting to be a part of. During one of our meetings, I was showing a presentation on the large monitor in the conference room. I had my hair in a ponytail—something that I had done from time to time. As I turned my head to look at the screen, the next thing I knew the CEO had grabbed my ponytail and used it to move my head! I felt mortified, infuriated and, as a woman, valueless instead of valuable.

Up until then, he'd always been a good boss, encouraging and keen to get the best out of his people. Everyone felt that he knew where the business was going, that he held its vision safe and that he'd always look out for all of us staff. Then there were problems; some were financial (sales had fallen a bit in that fiscal period) and others were personal—apparently his wife had left and was divorcing him. He began to pick on people, blame them—some subtle stuff at first, but then progressively nastier.

Two weeks later, I was in a meeting with five colleagues and the same guy came in. 'Everyone having a good time?' he asked, and then grabbed my ponytail so that my head nodded. Then he stroked my face.

I shouted 'Get off!' and he just said, 'If you have a problem, why don't you come sit on my lap and tell me all about it?'

I was humiliated. I noticed that he had a big clump of my hair in his fist. People laughed awkwardly. I was crying. He just sprinkled the torn hair over my head. I resigned."

25

TEERAPAT, FISHERMAN
BANGKOK, THAILAND

> Thou art a slave, whom fortune's tender arm
> With favour never clasp'd; but bred a dog.
>
> *Timon of Athens*, Act IV, Scene 3

"This is difficult for me... Thank you... Well, where to start? I will have to speak slowly...

Slavery is hidden under the carpet these days, but it exists still. I was forced to work for no pay for years at a time, under threat of extreme violence in the production of seafood. We were bought and sold like animals and held against our will on fishing boats off the coast... fishing for prawns, or shrimp, as the Americans call them. They were sold all over the world to big businesses... yes, and to supermarkets.

All the fishing boats had slaves working on them. Were we slaves? Well, we couldn't leave if we wanted to, that was for sure. So, yes, slaves. I was lucky. I escaped. We did 20-hour shifts, suffered regular beatings. Yes. Some of us were at sea for years; some were regularly given drugs... methamphetamines... to keep us going. There was torture and sometimes execution-style killings. Some say they saw people murdered in front of them.

I had friends who paid brokers to help them find work in other countries, in factories or on building sites. But they were sold instead to boat captains, sometimes for very little money. I thought I was going to die. They kept me chained up, they didn't care about me or give me much food…

I read the papers. I know supermarkets admit that they buy from companies that use slave labour, but nobody does anything. They just turn away their heads. The supply chain works in this way: slave ships fish and scoop up big quantities of little fish, fish that nobody wants… yes … inedible fish. This fish is sold to factories, where it is ground down into fishmeal and passed to companies that farm prawns. Those companies sell prawns to supermarkets. Supermarkets sell… to you.

Someone told me that over 20 million men, women and children are slaves in the world. I don't know. That's a lot of people—sold like property… and forced to work under threat of harm, or death. In all of these places there are chiefs, big people who manage and run the businesses, people who are in control—on the boats, in the plants, in the packaging places, in the factories, in the supermarkets. There is always someone in charge. Who challenges these people? Who says, 'You are doing this. Killing people, ruining people?'"

PART TWO

THE EVIL EXECUTIVE

Of course, women as well as men can be evil incarnate. For the purposes of this book, the evil executive is referred to as 'he', but be in no doubt that 'she' would apply just as much. The other thing to note is that the evil executive is referred to throughout the narrative often as a particular level of employee. Well, the person who is causing pain may not be an executive, of course—he could be a director, an associate, a supervisor or a colleague, a CEO, a boss, a manager, the proprietor—anyone who is worthy of the title 'evil' in your work environment.

There is another thing. While it is easy to offer comfort or advice, the position in which someone finds himself when confronted with evil at work is often very hard to describe. Vocabulary is inadequate. Bear in mind (and this is no solace) that with every positive suggestion in what follows, there is often an 'on the other hand'. Evil is difficult to overcome and the damage can truly be hard to limit.

26

LET'S BE CLEAR: WHAT IS THE EVIL EXECUTIVE LIKE?

> To thine own self be true.
>
> *Hamlet*, Act I, Scene 3

There are people in workplaces everywhere who are often described as difficult, narcissistic, vicious and with passive-aggressive personalities. In order to survive in these workplaces, a person must recognize the behavioural characteristic of these toxic personalities and learn how to deal with them. Unfortunately, it is not always easy to do anything. Also, the toxic behaviour of one person may be symptomatic of more serious dysfunction in the company.

In order to apply the label 'toxic', behaviours have to be pervasive, meaning that they must occur much or most of the time, and have the potential to cause serious damage in the work environment—and to individuals. A lack of empathy can be the root cause of toxicity. Empathy is the ability to identify what someone else is thinking or feeling and to respond to that person's thoughts and feelings with an appropriate emotion. People who lack empathy see other people as mere objects.

And then there's the organization itself and its history and mores. Does it confront aggressive people about inappropriate behaviour? Does it warn extreme bullies about dealing appropriately with others and adhering to company values? Does it manage complaints fairly and properly? Does it investigate charges? If your organization does these things, consider yourself fortunate. You are probably in a healthy environment. On the other hand, do your senior people turn a blind eye to harmful behaviour? Do they in any way encourage or reward disgraceful behaviour? When individuals are targeted and damaged, does the organization let that run, or does it do something fast? Does an evil executive usually get his way? Is bullying behaviour the norm rather than the exception?

Even if you aren't directly the victim of maliciousness, the atmosphere within the organization will probably affect you and it won't be a constructive environment in which to work. You may of course have no choice but to stay there, but most people have the option to leave. The dominant culture of the workplace has a huge impact on the ability to effectively deal with an evil executive. And you can't easily fight widespread anger, perpetual discontent, dysfunctional processes, broken relationships, non-functional meetings, hypocrisy and restrictive practices. Not on your own, anyway. In a toxic organization, upper management will often have allowed attitudes and policies to develop that have in turn created an environment favourable to the evil executive and hostile to everyone else. Including you.

In smaller organizations, evil executives often thrive when the owner, senior director or general manager isn't involved on a day-to-day basis. His or her remoteness from employees gives free rein to an evil executive. In larger companies, a rigid hierarchy may create a similar degree of remoteness, particularly when managers restrict communication in an upward direction. Even if management proudly claims an open-door policy, managers are possibly unreceptive to complaints about disgraceful behaviour. Also, if you tackle them about a problem, they may label *you* as a troublemaker. In a toxic environment, top executives may have been isolated for so long that they have stopped caring about their employees' well-being. It is seemingly irrational for management to ignore the morale of people upon whom the company's performance depends. But irrationality is no stranger to many organizations.

Many top executives rise to their position through evil practice. When they then see others using the same tactics, they are often impressed. They welcome the evil executive as one of their kind. They admire their many 'qualities' and invite him to join the elite. Once such an executive becomes part of the management group, it takes a near disaster to weaken that power. If anyone threatens the group, the members close ranks, and if you complain about a serious issue, they treat *you* as the problem: you are called disruptive, not a team player, divisive or a troublemaker. If you are in a toxic workplace and none of your efforts to change the toxic culture are successful, then you are probably better off just acknowledging that the people in charge are selfish and have limited caring capacity—and go find a healthier place to work. This is by no means always an option, of course.

When low morale becomes an issue in a business, an organization's managers will often address the symptoms rather than the underlying problem, i.e. the evil executive. Their objective is to satisfy employees that they are dealing with morale issues, but without causing the executive in question to leave the organization—either from their own fear or because they genuinely believe that he is an asset. Sometimes the executive's aggressive or manipulative behaviour is regarded as not being a problem at all, and that these issues are all about tough and firm management and, heaven help us, are absolutely necessary. Furthermore, senior management may acknowledge only one or two incidents of toxic behaviour and ignore the overall destructive pattern. Or they mislabel behaviours with euphemisms, for example characterizing manipulation as persuasion.

Firing people is often described in euphemistic terms. We can be 'let go', or find that we've been 'reorganized', 'displaced', suffered 'career upgrading', or 'right-sized'. At other times we're 'redeployed', subjected to 'transitioning' or discover that we're not 'strategic'. At other times we can be 'restructured', 're-engineered', 'employment challenged' and offered the opportunity to 'spend more time with our families' as part of a reduction in force.

Managers operating in turbulent environments need to make hard choices that often have undesirable consequences. Managers firing others to ensure business survival often have to use rationalization processes (e.g. 'it's not my fault') to help them cope with the consequences of their actions. By fixing the blame on others or on circumstances, not only are the executive's own injurious actions excusable, but he can, and will, feel justified in the process. This is not to say that firing people necessitates the person doing the firing is evil—not at all. But the point is that, as we shall see, the evil executive is clever and will use anything and anyone to get what he wants, under the cover of doing something that can be justified to and by management.

Greed can also be a very strong motivator. People with lots of money usually want more. When a company treats profits as the only focus, ethics and values often suffer. In this environment, malevolent behaviour is often tolerated—or even praised—if it appears to lead to higher profits or improved financial results. Of course, as we see from the media, and maybe from our own experiences, even though profits and benefits can be increased in the short term, over several years low morale and high staff turnover usually produce the opposite result. Experienced managers can allow themselves to become victims—at least temporarily—of a skilled manipulator. And if they allow the business to be ruined, they may become permanent victims themselves.

Ultimately, senior managers will likely suffer from their decision to allow a bully to thrive. Insolvency, bankruptcy, PR backlash and lawsuits are common in the wake of an evil executive's actions. However, a skilled evil executive can adapt to the organization's culture in a way that makes his destructive behaviours virtually undetectable to those around him—apart from his chosen targets. Perhaps over time he will ruin enough people for his true character to become widely known, but it is more likely that he will cause the termination of anyone who speaks up. So how can you fight this toxicity?

27

WHAT CAN BE DONE? NOT MUCH...

> Nothing will come of nothing:
> speak again.
>
> *King Lear*, Act I, Scene 1

This is not a cynical piece of advice. Sometimes, the situation is unbelievably awful, but it may just pass. Of course you may not want to let it just pass, and that's understandable. And doing nothing does not in any way obviate the need to discuss the problem with someone in authority who will listen; but it could be that the evil executive may leave, may be treading ever thinner ground, or may be losing power or support within the organization.

If you are able to look at the executive as a person, seeing his strengths and weaknesses, good traits (if any), you are now ready to understand them—not excuse them or accept them, but understand them a bit more. Such people are who they are and it's not your job to change them, even if you could. No matter what you do, they are unlikely to change as much as you'd like—if at all. Change only happens when a person wants to change. It is not within your control.

Maturity, in part, means accepting things for what they are. Wasting time being angry at the sky for being blue is crazy. So why waste time being angry with an executive who is harmful to others or to you? Why should you wait to find out? Tolerating abuse is never acceptable. But people can't always easily walk away from a job. And acceptance doesn't mean smiling while someone hurts you. You should defend yourself and take actions to improve the situation.

Here's a thing that can help to make you a bit happier. Never accept a monkey on your shoulder. Monkeys? People like depositing problems on other people. What on earth does this mean and what's it got to do with monkeys? Well, visualize a monkey, maybe two or even three. Each monkey represents a serious concern, a trouble, an aggravation, a problem, a nasty something that is an irritation, a concern. And somebody has given you the monkey and you've accepted it. Maybe you felt obliged to accept it. Maybe you felt that you had no choice but to accept it. Well, if someone gives you a problem or tells you that your work stinks over and over, imagine that each issue is a monkey and that it's been put on your shoulder and won't move. But that doesn't mean you have to keep these monkeys. They are not lovely and cuddly. They are nasty. They are not yours at all, so get rid of them. Don't accept them. Give them back. If you don't, then the annoying, anguish-causing monkeys will continue to irritate. Don't accept monkeys. Tell the owner that you won't accept the problem. Easy to say, hard to do. But, know this: when it works, you will feel better.

28

KNOW THE DIFFERENCE BETWEEN BULLYING AND EVIL

> These violent delights have
> violent ends
>
> *Romeo and Juliet*, Act II, Scene 6

Bullying at work is extremely serious and it's nasty for anyone who has been on the receiving end of it. But remember that we're talking about more than bullying. Of course, there will always be a certain amount of aggressive behaviour, even in the most benign of working environments. Conflict is endemic in many environments. But vitriolic and psychotic behaviour brings a different dimension.

For some, a job is a job, and that's it. For others a job is a passion. We're all different and want different things from life and have different ways of achieving these things. When our interests and ambitions are similar to the interests of our colleagues, all's well; but sometimes they are not. When these competing interests collide, as they inevitably will sometimes, the result is conflict, even if it's mild. This can lead to various levels of fear, frustration, jealousy, confusion, anger and fatigue. Perhaps we should be surprised, not that there is so much aggression in organizations and workplaces, but that there is so little.

On top of this, executive leaders have added pressure. Whether they are heading armies, companies, huge conglomerates, high street stores, governments, political parties or charities, the role of leaders is to guide us when we are in unfamiliar territory. That's their role, their job. Political, social, economic, educational and technical environments are changing all the time. To be a leader is to be constantly dealing with unfamiliar and uncertain situations. When people are at the top of the work ladder, there are few others to whom they can really refer; they are more or less alone. Sounding authoritative and confident is usually easier when one is in a supporting role, based on the solid ground of our level of competence. Leaders, though, spend much of their time dealing with uncertainty and making decisions in areas where they have perhaps little or no experience. Many leaders have to spend most of their time outside their comfort zones. It's hardly surprising, therefore, that they will occasionally lose their tempers. Some people are better at managing their discomfort (or tempers) than others. Leaders who regularly blow off steam are those for whom the uncertainty and insecurity sometimes get too much. But that doesn't make them evil.

Bad-tempered and aggressive behaviour, then, is an occasional but normal aspect of any workplace. To label all of it as evil, or even bullying, is to miss the essence of what makes evil behaviour so terrifying. A boss who rants and raves because he is frustrated or frightened, is quite different from one who regularly uses aggressive and violent behaviour as a so-called management tool. It might sometimes feel the same when you are on the receiving end, but there is a crucial difference between someone expressing their frustration and immoral behaviour.

If your boss shouts at everyone, regardless of their position in the hierarchy, he may be (let's stress *may* be) just a rather unpleasant man who can't control his temper—a moderate bully, perhaps. If he is obsequious to senior executives, but overbearing to more junior staff, then you are looking at someone who uses aggression and intimidation as a control strategy, but that's not necessarily evil, despite the fact that it's not palatable. If your boss targets certain people for especially severe criticism on a regular basis, then you have a bully in your organization. Where physical or permanent harm is involved, then that is an example of evil.

It's interesting to note that when an evil corporate executive is caught out and is publicly shown to be what he is, that person often appears meek and mild. People often wonder what all the fuss is (or was) about. Evil requires safety and victims. When both have gone, the balloon is pricked.

Aggression, even when it is targeted, is much easier to deal with than some of the less overt forms of bullying. An occasional shouting, swearing executive is obvious; you can see him coming and so, of course, can everyone else. You'll have plenty of evidence if you want to confront him. Much more difficult to deal with are the silent, nasty and 'invisible' evil executives. These people systematically exploit conflict and people's weaknesses, time and time again, below the radar. This type of behaviour is insidious. The effects creep up on you. Whether the evil is surreptitious or in your face, colleagues pick up on the hidden message that you are 'out of favour' and start to avoid you. Often, the first concrete evidence is when your boss starts muttering about poor performance and you don't get a pay rise or a share of a bonus. The menace grows and becomes personal and long-lasting—and public. This sort of attack is often like having a slowly dripping water leak in your house. By the time you find out what is happening, the damage is done. Some would sooner face the ranting and swearing menace any day. At least you can defend yourself—even a little—when the aggressor is in front of you.

Over the next few years, round the world, we may see a lot more aggressive behaviour in organizations. Uncertain times and unfamiliar challenges make people feel scared. People become concerned about job safety. And there is a whole generation of people who have only known good times. They either don't remember the last deep recession, or were too junior to be responsible for managing its consequences. Some who were never affected by job insecurity may have zero empathy with anyone who was. Many have no experience of trying to deliver the same services with rapidly shrinking budgets, of having to tell people, for the third year running, that there will be no pay rise and having to make large numbers of jobs redundant. For some of these people without jobs, this will translate into aggressive behaviour. But this is what happens in economic cycles—and that may be awful, but isn't necessarily evil.

The most likely reason for evil behaviour is that the evil executive wants to be controlling all of the time. Some will tell you that they're tough or demanding because they have high standards but, where evil is concerned, that's just an excuse. An evil executive enjoys belittling, berating and harming employees to cover up his own insecurities. The evil executive may scream at or humiliate employees to make them feel incompetent, and go out of his way to place blame on others, no matter what the consequences. An evil executive will have zero empathy for anyone else's issues or problems, no matter how serious.

Be very sure that you are not confusing normal behaviour (even if it's a bit discomfiting) with a really evil scenario. While some people may be able to perform effectively under a tough boss, there are many who will crumble under the consistent pressure of trying to meet demands. That poses different problems, but it's life, and not necessarily a toxic, evil scenario.

Obviously we all perform best in a happy, safe, healthy environment. To make an environment toxic actually takes very little effort (which is why clever evil executives succeed) and can only be borne for a while before output falls, objectives are lost and the smell of fear, stress and mistrust pervades the workplace. And that impacts people's ability to effectively complete even mundane tasks, or even to think straight. The organization experiences a decrease in employee commitment, a rise in absenteeism, an increase in errors and poor-quality work, as well as increased interpersonal conflicts and team dysfunction.

An executive who is demanding in his legitimate expectation of high performances is simply doing his job, provided that the feedback he offers is professional. The tough manager wants to drive performance, but he may come across as overbearing and unfair. The evil executive is different, however. He is envious of others and is threatened by their competence or likability. He hates anything that is 'wrong' in physical appearance. He seeks to gain and keep control by undermining others. He manifests a focused pattern of aggression, abusing his power through repeated efforts to intentionally threaten and ruin his victim, or manipulates the victim for his own purposes. Intending to inflict harm, he uses aggressive tactics that are repeated, long-lasting, damaging and increase in severity.

To reiterate, then: make sure you have not confused 'demanding' with 'evil'. There are lots of demanding bosses out there who insist that you do the job you are paid to do. Why wouldn't they? Why wouldn't you? If you are not qualified to do that job or cannot do the job for some reason, the problem is actually yours. Nobody likes to be told that they are less than good. Examine yourself and your situation and do all you can to deliver what's required. If you have delivered on time and as promised, and if your boss is still unpleasant to you, sit down and talk to him. Maybe you have missed the point of something, or maybe you do have room for improvement. Maybe you're not as good as you think you are. Take it all on board and consider carefully what is said. The boss might learn something, too, and might manage you better. It doesn't always happen like that, but it happens.

29

THE STRATEGY OF TALKING

> Speak the speech, I pray you,
> as I pronounced it to you,
> trippingly on the tongue.
>
> *Hamlet*, Act III, Scene 2

An obvious strategy is to inform higher management of your difficulties in working with someone, particularly a senior someone. Your chances of success using this approach are not encouraging. Why? Well, for a couple of reasons. First, because high-level management, in all likelihood, was responsible for employing or promoting the executive in the first place, and may be hesitant to admit their mistake. Second, the executive has, again in all probability, already informed his or her own manager about the difficulty of working with you and, thus, your reputation has been established and sullied. Where there was no doubt, there now is. People can't easily remove that which others have falsely put in their ears. This happens all the time. Say something to someone about someone else and the likelihood is they will retain that image. If it is repeated by others, then it begins to stick.

Ultimately, a strategy of talking to the evil executive's seniors often fails because it ignores a truism about conflict: a rational approach (such as conversation and logic) to resolve an irrational situation (such as threats and violence by an evil executive) is rarely successful. A healthy relationship requires both individuals to be willing and able to address the inevitable challenges; if one person is uninterested in doing so, then it's an exercise in futility and disappointment. The conflict remains.

Most of us hate conflict at work or, for that matter, anywhere. Most of us are adept at dodging conflicts, but that merely delays what will become worse as time goes on. What is important is trying to do something about it here and now. That doesn't mean that facing up to evil behaviour will make it go away—it probably won't. Evil behaviour isn't rational. It's psychotic. But talking constructively is worth the effort, although it may be that you'll have to try several times. Remember that a psychotic person is someone who could be regarded as bordering on insane. This is not a normal state of mind and, be warned, trying to have a normal conversation with an evil executive may get you nowhere. Worse, it could make the situation even worse.

Winning a conflict, i.e. getting the outcome you want, can be gratifying, sure, but the problem is that the underlying issue has not been solved if both sides don't feel comfortable. The problem will simply reappear later over some other topic. So, much better than winning a conflict is resolving it. And that involves both talking and listening.

Particularly when a workplace is changing and new ideas are being developed and implemented, conflict is inevitable. There can be no business or organizational change without some conflict. The trick is to make sure that you also have no conflict without change, because that is the truly dangerous thing: conflicts that go on for years with all parties refusing to budge an inch.

It's very tempting to wait for a conflict to blow over by itself, but it rarely does—in most cases it only becomes compounded or swept under the carpet. Most conflicts at work do not come from something that was said, but from something that wasn't. It's tempting to try and smooth things over and pretend everything is normal. Don't. That's the most common reason why conflicts at work escalate: nobody does anything. Everyone's waiting for the other person (or people) to admit fault.

Many of you will have walked into a new job, only to find that there has been something of a constant 'war' between this person and that person, or this department against that department, since the year dot—and now the conflict has become part of the organizational process. It may be unpleasant to tackle the issue straight away, but it gets even more unpleasant after the conflict has festered over time. Conflict, though, doesn't mean that the environment is evil, or even that there is anyone evil involved in the conflict. Stupidity, stubbornness, ambition, lack of teamwork skills and a host of other factors may have played a part. But, within an atmosphere of conflict, an evil executive may find a golden opportunity to use the environment for his own devious and toxic purposes.

In the early stages of a conflict, the most powerful tool for resolving it is to simply ask to discuss the issue. If somebody has done something that made you angry, upset or hurt in any way, if you don't understand somebody's viewpoint, if you don't understand his actions—ask. Do it nicely, difficult though that may be. 'Hi. I was wondering why you did xyz yesterday' or 'I've noticed that you often do abc. Why is that?' are examples. 'Why the bloody hell do you always have to xyz?' is less constructive and not helpful. Sometimes there's a perfectly good reason why that person does what he does, and a potential conflict evaporates right there as long as it is explained.

As mentioned, there's a difference between people just being human versus real venomous intent. Never assume that people do what they do to annoy or spite you. People typically have a good reason to act as they do, even the things that really get on your nerves. Never assume bad faith on anyone else's part. However, given what you've read so far, it's likely that you'll know the difference between trying to talk reasonably to an executive who is likely to listen and someone who is unlikely to listen at all.

If you're certain that an evil executive is harming you, then do try and talk to him. If you feel like the person is just itching to pounce on the slightest mistake you make then you should try and talk. If he has no good reason to be disgusting in his behaviour towards you—if he is racist, if he is personal, if he harasses you—then try inviting him to a meeting. A hurried conversation at your desk between emails and phone calls won't solve anything, even if you are allowed to get to that point. You need an undisturbed location and time to address the issue. If you feel you need someone with you, try that—although it is less likely to work, since the evil executive may not want a witness. And make no mistake, offering this invitation to talk may be the hardest part of the whole process. It can be remarkably hard to take that first step. The obvious negative is if the executive refuses to meet you, or will meet you, but won't discuss the issue at hand. Then you can offer the invitation again or put on record to someone senior that you're trying to manage a situation; but then you may get little support from anyone on high. All not easy.

If you do get a short face-to-face meeting, you need a way to structure the conversation. If it develops into a blame scenario, you won't win. Your tormentor will just deflect accusations or suggestions that he is doing something wrong. And put the blame on you. So, it's important that you prepare the meeting thoroughly and write down notes for each step, so that you know what you're going to say and what you want to achieve. However, don't for goodness' sake read from your notes. That would irritate anyone. Do him the courtesy of knowing what it is you're talking about—no matter how nervous you are. After each of the steps that you want to cover in the meeting, ask the other person if he agrees with your thinking and if he'd like to add anything. Keep it as formal or informal as you feel sits within your comfort zone.

Another tactic in such a meeting is to identify the problem as you see it, but do remember not to make accusations. Be neutral and objective. If he begins to make personal comments about you, try and ignore this—difficult as that will be. His language and tone may become hurtful and abusive. But try to get him to recognize a situation that is causing you difficulty and pain, particularly if that involves any abuse. Describe the facts of the situation as objectively as possible. What is actually happening? When and how did it happen? What was the reason? You should only cite observable facts and not guess at what the other person is thinking or doing. You can say, 'I've noticed that you're always criticizing me at meetings and telling people I'm stupid,' because that's an observable fact. You shouldn't say, 'I've noticed that you've stopped respecting my ideas,' because that assumes something that can't be verified as true.

Think carefully. If you have something for which you should apologize, then do. But only if it is a real issue. Don't apologize for being Muslim, Jewish, fat, thin, short, tall, educated, poor, bald, blue-eyed—whatever. These are simply facts: why should you apologize, unless you are doing something that is not part of company rules or that is unsociable? But do apologize if you believe that you may have done something to offend the evil executive in the first place. This may not solve much, but it may stop the executive from picking on you in the future. Maybe.

Whatever happens in any discussion, remember that you're not accepting the entire blame, but you're taking responsibility for your contribution to the situation (if you did indeed contribute). Tell the executive why it's worth it to you (and to him and the organization) to solve the conflict. Again this might work, or it might exacerbate the situation—but it's worth a try. It can be difficult, because few people find it easy to appreciate a person they hate or who has done awful things. Similarly, if the executive genuinely hates you (for whatever reason about which you may or may not know), then it's unlikely that he will change his view after one meeting.

Importantly, try and discuss what the conflict has meant for you and the organization, and explain your view as to why that's a problem. Outlining the consequences of the conflict shows why it's necessary to resolve it. It also helps participants to look beyond themselves and see the conflict 'from the outside'. In any conversation of this type, it is critical to set a goal, so both of you know the outcome for which you're aiming. It also makes reaching the outcome a lot more likely and possible. And, if the discussion is going well, ask for specific actions that can be implemented right away. Even a small change may help you, and maybe make your working life easier. Don't go into the meeting with assumptions; focus on reality and keep emotion out, hard as that will undeniably be. If you reach agreement for even a tiny change, then take it and you can say that you've been successful—for the moment.

However, none of this may make the slightest bit of difference if the evil executive believes that he has no need to alter his behaviour, or simply chooses not to because nobody is making him.

30

CONFLICT HURTS

> Cry 'Havoc!' and let slip the dogs of war,
> That this foul deed shall smell above the earth
> With carrion men, groaning for burial
>
> *Julius Caesar*, Act III, Scene 1

Conflict is often assessed as measuring risk against reward to estimate the value of pursuing a problem. This basically means: is it worth it? Wherever danger or evil is present, the fear of injury or worse can be a hugely debilitating factor. Most of us have an aversion to conflict and most of us are uncomfortable with it. The result is an implied understanding, supported by most societies and therefore by most organizations, whereby the general population allows potential points of conflict to simply pass by. It happens every day—in the car, on the street, on a bus, on a train, by the water-cooler, in a store, at home. But letting evil prosper can lead to greater terror, not less—as history has shown time and time again.

As we all know, the word 'conflict' implies some sort of fight, battle or struggle. It's more than an argument, which is an exchange of diverging views. A conflict is more of a very serious disagreement, often a protracted one, where things are said and done that are not normal for the protagonists. Language is basic and full of accusation, and bodies ready themselves for a physical fight. An evil executive will want people to see things the way he sees things—period. To repeat, problems of conflict usually won't disappear of their own accord.

Depressing as that sounds, if you're staying in an organization, you must do something to alleviate the situation. If the evil executive has hurt you mentally or physically, refused to acknowledge your work, derided you—whatever—just remember to have some solutions ready. As mentioned, know what you want to achieve. Also, you don't want to go to someone senior with petty or interpersonal matters that you are expected to resolve yourself. Remember that.

When conflict occurs in the workplace, it can reduce morale, lower work productivity, increase absenteeism and cause large-scale confrontations that can, in turn, lead to serious and violent crimes. Conflict is painful. Evil executives are often very frightening, shocking, embarrassing—and far too often tolerated. We don't want to have to deal with them, whether we are the target or not. We want to keep our heads down. We want to avoid trouble. We don't want the battle or the hurt. So we either pretend these people aren't creating hell, or we tolerate them and the hell. We all want safety, we all want to belong and we all want to matter. Often, these things are exactly what the evil executive wants too, on a bigger scale, but he is trying to get it in an inappropriate way. And he will, indeed, probably get his way.

No matter how hard an individual may try to resolve an issue, it might not get resolved. This is not meant to depress you, but it is a fact. The issue may not go away and instead may escalate to a point of no return. Which is exactly what the evil executive and his cohorts want. What could have been resolved through goodwill and the appropriate mechanisms in place now becomes a contest. Some of the accusations and demeaning attacks by the evil executive may be guided by the need for a scapegoat, the need for personal power over others and by personal animosities, fears or jealousies. It's evil at work.

And the sad thing, as we've seen, is that this kind of behaviour might be ignored, tolerated, misinterpreted or actually instigated by the company or the organization's management as a deliberate strategy. Of course, any victim will feel exhausted and incapable of defending himself or herself, let alone initiating action, legal or otherwise. But the truth is that this kind of heavy-duty conflict can only continue as long as it's allowed to. Organizational leadership plays the most important part in its prevention. By enforcing and ensuring decency and high ethical and social standards in the workplace and by creating a positive environment, evil will struggle to prosper.

31

BE COMPETENT AND DO YOUR JOB WELL

> We know what we are,
> but know not what we may be.
>
> *Hamlet*, Act IV, Scene 5

The one attribute that will most likely determine success or failure in life is the ability to be a good person, one who is kind-hearted, controls the most destructive of human emotions, tells the truth, does what's right and always looks for the good in everything. That person makes home and work fun, and is convinced that people yearn for happiness in their lives. In work, the 'good' person instils a sense of adventure, excitement and, where required, calm—and that leads to loyalty, commitment and productivity. Life isn't always like that, of course, and we don't all have bosses or colleagues that fall into that category. Nor are we all like that, either—often not even close, alas.

Many, when confronted with an evil executive, feel that they may be doing something terribly wrong, or fear that they are doing their job badly. It probably isn't true but actually, whether it is or isn't, you must be absolutely competent in your work—as far as you can be. This requires considerable effort and is stressful, but if you are doing your job well, then it doesn't give anyone an opportunity to highlight your errors and mistakes. (Although, of course, if the evil executive wants to criticize anything small or large, true or false, then he will.) Highlighting errors and mistakes in and of itself is not evil—that's just management, and necessary if warranted.

Try to establish a reputation across the company. Avoid allowing the evil executive to define your reputation; it certainly won't be good. Instead, you define it. Build a wide array of contacts at all levels, both inside and outside work. You may establish a reputation for positive performance and attitude. This may even distance the evil executive and his cohorts. Be aware that the evil executive may try and make your life even more miserable. After all, you are (in his eyes) making him look 'bad', and he won't like that.

So, prepare your CV or résumé, broaden your network of contacts and begin a job search. With some luck, your work situation will improve and your job search will have been premature; in all likelihood, though, your job search will be a good investment for a better future.

32

THE QUEST FOR GOODNESS

> Virtue is bold and goodness
> never fearful.
>
> *Measure for Measure*, Act III, Scene 1

This part is not at all meant to be holier than thou, and neither is it about religions or faiths. Many will undoubtedly have worked in and with organizations that seem to cultivate and reward more than their fair share of villains, thugs and hoodlums, masquerading as leaders, colleagues and managers. It is undoubtedly difficult to find the good in an organization when there's no visible sign of positive values in action—the sign might be on the wall outlining the company's vision, but other than that, nothing. The words have no teeth or real meaning; they hang and gather dust.

Some of an organization's leaders may just like to be surrounded by enforcers. Some employees whose shoulders are bowed under the weight of evil tolerate a truly heinous individual because in management's words, they 'like to have a Rottweiler in the office looking out for our interests'. Said lightly and meant seriously. Sometimes, the organization's senior leaders appear to enjoy conflict and commit the 'dogs of war' to enforce various 'rules' that you'll never see written down. If you think that this sounds like a criminal gang, then it is just that. And they may see this approach as entertaining—it fits their 'survival of the fittest' view of the world. They see it as creative and helpful to the organization's dynamics. This is not an uncommon situation. Some executives might be so preoccupied with their own issues that they are truly blind to the carnage going on around them—and, in truth, they may not care. In fact, knowing that they are causing pain might be giving them a big high, a thrill. We know that there are some who find the infliction of pain much like a drug. Inflicting pain is not the preserve of street hoodlums, bank robbers or mindless scum who go around beating up pensioners.

Being a decent person is about having a positive mental attitude. But the negativity bias does fight us. How do we sustain a good attitude? Sometimes, being good is about being brave and standing up if we think something goes against the organization's values. Treating other people with respect and not letting ourselves get squashed are examples of acting for the good. Good is being clear in our communication. People feel good if they have high-enough self-esteem to say that they want something, but if the other person can't give it, that's fine too. It's about being assertive without being aggressive. It's about being responsible for ourselves and being able to manage an adult relationship with other people. Ultimately, being a good person is not about over-giving. It's about putting others first when necessary. In everyday life, being a good person is about serving others just as much as yourself. It's about care and it's about decency.

We are familiar with large-scale atrocities throughout the world: genocide, war, murder, child abuse, theft, and so on. We are shocked—or most of us are—and we feel helpless. On a personal level, we've all been wronged one way or another over time. It's hard to see the good in someone when they just lied to you or cheated on you. At work, when someone does something shocking, horrifying or terrifying, that, too, beggars belief. Suddenly wickedness is on your doorstep. It's in your face and your stomach dissolves.

In considering the evil executive, we have a person with a label. Such a label is not an intrinsic feature of the person; it's merely a useful way of describing him. We can and should challenge labels—our own and those attributed by other people. We do tend to accept labels far too readily. So, if we don't make ready judgments about people, how do we assess the evil executive? It's pretty clear from the discussion so far that an evil executive is someone who will repeatedly do things that are abhorrent, unjust and toxic, things that any normal person would not do, or even think of doing. The labelling comes from repeated actions, not just a one-off.

33

CONTAMINATION

> Now is the winter of our discontent.
>
> *Richard III*, Act I, Scene 1

Some evil executives spread contamination quietly and slowly, while others smugly manipulate their colleagues, using them as instruments for their own success. That causes toxicity. Regardless of their methods, evil executives cause irrevocable damage to their organizations and employees by hindering performance and creating unnecessary stress on a seismic scale.

Many managers will argue that they are there to produce results of some sort and that any solution to achieving that end is justified. Many in senior positions in armies and businesses say that they are 'just obeying orders'. Is this a justifiable excuse?

While the best option when you have a bad boss is to seek other employment, this isn't always possible. Successful people often know how to make the most of a bad situation. In order to decontaminate an office of negativity, there are some approaches, but do note that these may not be possible for everyone. It is one thing to dislike your job, but it is quite another to feel physically ill and truly terrified when going to work. If your job has no redeeming qualities, your work environment may be toxic in more ways than one—and possibly caused by an evil executive. A toxic work environment is anywhere where the work, the atmosphere and the behaviours leave you so dismayed, so perpetually anxious and fearful, that it seems that it might make you ill. Make no mistake, every job annoys and distresses at some point, no matter what level you hold in an organization. But you know an environment is full of terror when you can't find joy in anything there. The only good thing about your job is the end of the day—and each hour as it passes. If any of this sounds familiar, it's time to do something.

What are the overall signs of a toxic workplace? Widespread anger and huge frustration, somewhere where the evil executive is admired, where scapegoats are always blamed, where relationships are dysfunctional, where hypocrisy is obvious, where systems are onerous and where HR is incompetent or powerless. A toxic environment is one where any efforts to make your company a better place to work seem superficial. Turnover is usually high in a toxic workplace, often with the most talented people leaving.

In a toxic environment, we've said that the evil executive is often admired by senior management, regardless of his tactics. Is he widely respected, despite inappropriate behaviour? When an evil executive loses control of his temper or intentionally embarrasses a subordinate, do others justify his actions as strong management, or even dismiss them as irrelevant, saying, 'Well, never mind—suck it up'? Toxic environments are also those where picking on and blaming others seems like a blood sport. In a toxic workplace, an evil executive 'explains' a mistake by castigating and accusing someone else. He thus avoids any responsibility or accountability for his actions. This habit of accusation can cause persistent problems. By not acknowledging his own role in causing mistakes, he finds or provides no answers that can prevent future mistakes.

Over time, high turnover allows the executive to blame a whole new set of scapegoats. Of course, 'old' scapegoats may continue to be blamed long, long after they've left the organization. Ring any bells? The evil executive can use two or three ex-employees to explain away a whole host of problems, since they are no longer around to explain how the protagonist was actually at fault. In a toxic team, department, division or organization, processes tend to be dysfunctional, particularly if the evil executive has helped create them in the first place. In this situation, procedures and processes don't make sense, making it difficult to get things done. Management reviews are an unnecessary burden and rarely happen; or, if they do, then with strong bias and with many reports that don't have any meaning. For any given task, the established process appears illogical. There are no clear objectives, so it can be tough to determine what's important and what isn't.

Toxicity may also mean that, at times, you find yourself buried in work that appears to be completely unnecessary and nobody can explain the purpose with any clear rationale. The evil executive routinely makes decisions that impact on you without telling you or seeking your input. Deadlines are never established based on logical scheduling of larger goals, but instead appear arbitrary and whimsical. There is no consideration for anyone else's commitments, time or home life. And often in toxic environments—and in order to create the impression that personnel issues are being addressed—senior management may perhaps set up a committee to investigate specific problems and suggest solutions—not necessarily against a person, but for the workplace at large. The results are frequently based on the often misplaced premise that the employees aren't very sophisticated and can be easily appeased or duped. Input from employees is discounted or ignored. Because the process is dysfunctional, the results are meaningless.

Let's say, for example, that such a committee is formed to investigate low morale. But since the workplace is toxic, the committee won't have the authority to investigate the executive who is causing the rot (even if he can be clearly identified). Even worse, that executive actually may be on the committee. Or the committee must first report to a high-level executive, who is a toxic executive or *the* toxic executive. And so it goes. This isn't paranoia, either. Since management may ignore the impact of toxicity on morale, they instead turn to 'creative' thinking. Perhaps they find some popular solution to 'make employees feel better'. This could include an award of some kind, competitions with no reason and no outcome, or away days on quad bikes in muddy fields in the name of developing teamwork. Not only do these 'solutions' fail to deal with (or curtail the activities of) the evil executive, but the premise is fatally flawed. By positing a pointless solution in the name of bolstering morale, staff will feel that they are being treated like idiots. The evil executive is winning.

In a toxic workplace, everyone seems to struggle with relationships. Misunderstandings are common, leading to frustration, anger, hopelessness, lethargy and inefficiency. Gossip and criticism are rife and become the norm, and cliques lead to favouritism and feuding. People go round in circles. Absent in a toxic environment are honest and straightforward conversations—both inside meetings and outside them. You rarely see a quick resolution of relationship issues and, indeed, bad feelings may linger for months—or even years. Bad feelings become worse feelings and then toxic. The evil executive who dominates meetings will trade in vague platitudes, instead of addressing real problems. He will focus on theory rather than dealing with reality. But it'll sound good. By ignoring the real problems facing the organization or individuals, he will fail to consider anything of substance. Apart, that is, from pursuing his own agenda.

The evil executive will likely dominate any conversation or group meeting at work or socially through his aggressive style, including giving monologues, arguing, criticizing, interrupting and invariably speaking louder than anyone else. He will always know best. Open discussions are stifled and progress impeded. He will use a meeting to embarrass, ridicule and humiliate his opponents and targets. In a toxic workplace, any complaints about the executive's domination of meetings, or anything else, will (as we know) likely fall upon deaf ears.

Toxicity at work nearly always includes hypocrisy on a wide scale. With hypocrisy often comes measures straight out of *The Emperor's New Clothes*, whereby the evil executive will fool his audiences into believing some mumbo jumbo management theses. Indeed, toxic executives often overcompensate by adopting faddish management approaches, as if propaganda is an effective tool to overcome reality. Well, that's worked before on a consistent basis in politics and throughout history. The result in an organization, as in a country or state, may be aggressively promoted organizational values that don't seem to match day-to-day realities. For example, clear communication is preached in elaborate seminars, while poor communication continues to be the norm. Valuing and respecting others is publicized in the company mission statement, but undermining and belittling staff seems pervasive. Everyone is told to make company goals their first priority and adopt a spirit of teamwork, but bitter and toxic competition dominates. Worst of all, the most consistent violators of company values are the most highly rewarded.

An evil executive can be quite outspoken in preaching company values, pressuring others to modify their behaviour in accordance with their detail, even as he consistently violates those very same values. Rather than being punished for his violations, the executive is rewarded for his outward pretensions of leadership. In the rare event that he is actually held to task for breaking company values, the process is ineffective and inevitably leads nowhere.

We know that an evil executive usually thrives by controlling others. He prefers a workplace with poor systems and processes that mean little, offering him more opportunities to tightly control others. Organizations fall into this mode of operation by designing and implementing overly detailed operational systems which are never properly understood by anyone, but are practised because that's the way it's always been done. Of course, the evil executive can be totally justified in creating and implementing his own systems. The systems—his rules—allow him to control the actions of others. And that leads to what he wants: power.

34

CHALLENGE

> Things bad begun make strong themselves by ill.
>
> *Macbeth*, Act III, Scene 2

This is not about you challenging an evil executive, because the likelihood is that at face value you won't win such a challenge—and, indeed, it will undoubtedly make matters considerably worse. No, this thought concerns the evil executive being challenged by other managers.

When challenged by more enlightened executives, an evil executive might explain that operational systems of his devising are absolutely necessary to maintain, say, discipline, productivity and quality control. He complains that without these systems and rules, employees would not be held accountable for their actions. He may launch into a long-winded description of a former company for which he has worked which used these systems, or he may refer to sophisticated management studies, offering false quotes and nonsense statistics to support his point.

In a toxic environment, human resource managers are often either unable or unwilling to deal with rampant workplace evil. Signs of an incompetent or powerless HR manager include an inability to respond effectively to damaging incidents, refusal to treat complaints as valid and significant—or criticizing the complainant without understanding the situation. The HR manager would perhaps rather avoid confrontation, so instead asks the complainant to change his/her own behaviour to accommodate the evil executive, with no recognition of the executive's destructive behaviour. If evil behaviour is actually acknowledged, there is no follow-up on requests for the executive to modify his approach—perhaps because the primary goal is to pacify the complainant, not change the executive. How can these (presumably) well-trained professionals fail to deal with evil? Well, a skilled liar and cheat can convince a naïve, or even a not so naïve, HR manager that their behaviour is fully justified by circumstances or by the failings of the complainant. In the end, the target, the victim (not always the complainant, of course) gets blamed either as the instigator or as a whinger and whiner. In this way, an HR manager can contribute to workplace toxicity.

An HR manager or other manager may also honour an evil executive's leadership in the company in much the same way that senior people within the organization do. If such an executive is already respected by senior management, confronting him carries huge risks for anyone, no matter at what level. It makes more sense to side with the evil executive, blaming the target or anyone else. When the manager, HR or otherwise, believes his own job may be at risk if he makes an enemy of a powerful evil executive, it's unlikely that you will see any meaningful action to address the problem.

In smaller organizations, evil executives often thrive when the owner isn't involved in day-to-day matters. His remoteness from employees gives free rein to the executive. In larger organizations, a rigid hierarchy may create a similar degree of remoteness, particularly when the top people haven't much of a clue as to what goes on 'down below' or on the shop floor. Even if executives shout out loud about an open-door policy, they're often unreceptive to complaints about dreadful and sadistic behaviour.

Many top executives rise to their position by stepping on others. When they see others using the same tactics, they are impressed. They welcome the evil executive, sometimes as one of their own kind. They may of course one day want to 'eliminate' him from the competition. But, they see force, or the threat of force, as being 'reasonable'. That keeps others in line, not just you. And it's extraordinarily hard to challenge.

35

FRIENDSHIP?

> Those friends thou hast,
> and their adoption tried,
> Grapple them unto thy soul
> with hoops of steel.
>
> *Hamlet*, Act I, Scene 3

This is an interesting conundrum if the evil executive becomes too friendly—and not in a fun, team-building sort of way. He is constantly inviting you to spend time outside of work and engages in unnecessary office gossip. He uses influence to make friends at the expense of his work. He chooses favourites and creates divisions among employees, who in turn become frustrated by the imbalance in attention and respect—and they, too, may turn vitriolic. The most important thing to do with this type of executive is to learn to set firm boundaries—if you can.

What does this mean? Well, don't allow his position of authority to intimidate you. By consciously and proactively establishing a boundary, you can take control of the situation. For example, you can remain friendly with the executive throughout the day, but still not be afraid to say no to drinks after work. Peer group pressure is a tough one and it's likely that the executive will have the group onside. The difficult part is maintaining consistency with your boundaries, even if the executive is persistent. There is, once again, another side to this. If you say no too many times, that might make you a victim and an 'antisocial' target.

There is another downside. In this case, you would need to be cautious because, as time goes on, there is a likelihood that the evil executive will bide his time and catch you alone on the basis that he thinks you're avoiding him. So a compromise might be to attend occasional social events, but always with others. Similarly, you might find yourself disenfranchised from your peers if they believe that you've become one of the evil executive's sidekicks. So be careful, either way.

36

IT'S IN THE DETAIL

> To do a great right, do a little wrong
> And curb this cruel devil of his will.
>
> *Merchant of Venice*, Act IV, Scene 1

An evil executive who is a micromanager makes you feel as if you are under constant surveillance—discomfiting at best and career-limiting at worst. He thinks that everything you do is wanting. He has contempt for much of what you do. Nothing you do is ever correct. There is always, but always, something that requires correction and, even when that correction has been effected, there's always something else that's not quite right or totally wrong. He will tell you this privately or in front of others. A whole report might be thrown in the bin and you're asked to rewrite it. And then when you do, it might be thrown away yet again. Or he may, in a pretence of exasperation, ask a colleague of yours to manage your work—or do it in order to humiliate you. The result is huge frustration and demotivation. The micromanager pays too much attention to small and mostly irrelevant details and his constant hovering makes employees feel discouraged, frustrated and extraordinarily uncomfortable.

A micromanager is naturally and positively drawn to the employee who produces work the way he envisages—even if that methodology is not the best. The challenge with the micromanager is grasping the 'envisioned way'. To do this, try asking specific questions about your project, check-in frequently and look for trends in the micromanager's feedback. There's usually a pattern.

The only way to stop the situation from getting worse is to take a stand against controlling, perfectionist behaviour as soon as you identify it. Most people have far less power over you than you think they do. This includes your micro-managing evil executive, who is metaphorically beating you with the hammer of incompetence.

Be wary. If you're in a situation where you think some-one is micromanaging you on a regular basis, then you're in trouble. Under these conditions, the illusion of control can become very powerful. If left unchecked, you will give up more and more control, and the other person will take more. The only way to break this cycle of apparent control is to challenge its existence. If you are able, stand up to the negative comments and any abuse that goes with them. Say no. You should do that politely and give your reasons. Keep emotion out of it. Stick to facts. But, of course, you also need to be clear of the distinction between your work, which may have genuine faults, and the micromanager's desire to control you.

Don't try to fix the micromanagers in your life. Don't waste your time trying to demonstrate to someone how controlling he or she is. They'll never see it, and neither will others. In any case, a psychotic manager is unlikely to be reasonable. Sometimes, you could aim to complete the work in the way that you believe your manager will approve, and make it clear that, until the due date for delivery, he should let you get on with it. Some controlling bosses might threaten you if you start to pull away. That's fine. Just keep a record of what's happening and discuss the issue with HR, or with someone else at a senior level. Don't fall victim to the illusion of control. Be as firm as you can.

If you aren't new to your job and you haven't done anything that would cause your manager to question your competence or trust, then look at how he manages others. If you aren't the only person he micromanages in a nasty, spiteful and harming way, then the issue, most likely, lies one hundred percent with him and you'll need to dig a little deeper. For example, maybe he is a new executive who has never undergone training in people management. Maybe a past employee made a mistake that harmed him in his career, and now he's trying to stop that happening again. Maybe he has an extreme analytical social style and enjoys being involved in all of the nitty-gritty—and he doesn't even realize how negatively staff experience his behaviour. Or he doesn't care. But with an evil executive, it may be all of these and then some—and there may be no rationale as far as anyone can see. Psychosis isn't rational—it is a severe mental disorder in which thought and emotions are so impaired that an awareness of reality is completely lost.

However, if the reason for the over-attention to detail is for genuine and explained management or individual reasons, then a dialogue is possible and evil doesn't come into it.

Meet with the executive, if you can, to discuss your concerns, and be ready to provide specific examples of his micromanaging habit and its negative impact on your productivity. Ask him, 'How can we best work together?' Try to establish a positive and reasonable working relationship by learning his leadership style and preferred method of operating and communicating—and then adapt yourself to working with that style. Agree on your goals, objectives, tasks and projects, and ask him for the freedom to try different methods to accomplish your work. He may well refuse (which is fair enough) because what you're suggesting is going against his grain. Find out the level of interaction he wants—it may actually be the better route.

The key to surviving an evil executive who is all over your work like a bad and itchy rash is to determine a mutually agreed balance between his need for information and involvement and your need for freedom to be productive.

Let's be clear, though: any action of attempted positivity is not likely to work on a corporate villain, a nasty soul, an extractor of oxygen—in other words, someone who will not listen to anything you are really saying, let alone do anything that would support you. With such a person, there is the agony and frustration of knowing the truth and being unable to do anything about changing it without the possibility of terrible consequences.

Remember that no action from you is likely to change the truly evil executive. Some will never stop searching for something to over-analyse and micromanage. And then it becomes personal and more psychotic. When this is the case, you must learn to derive your sense of satisfaction from within. Don't allow the executive's obsession with details to create feelings of inadequacy in you, as this will only lead to further stress and underperformance. If it still remains a nightmare, then seek another role in the business or leave.

37

EMOTIONS

> I am not of that feather to shake off
> My friend when he must need me.
>
> *Timon of Athens*, Act I, Scene 1

Emotions are not magic. Most people believe that they have very little control over how they feel. That may or may not be true. However, when we get in a mood, we often stay there until we feel that it's safe to come away from it, or the bubble is burst by a realization that we were silly or that the position was a stupid one to maintain. That much is normal. We make emotional decisions, often having to spend large amounts of time and energy correcting these decisions later. That, too, is normal.

But in an evil environment this impulse can work against us. Evil executives will get in our heads when we're in a bad mood and they will passive-aggressively push our buttons. That's how crowd mentality sometimes works, too. Or, the executive will use our fear of losing our job against us, to keep us doing precisely and only what he wants us to do.

Learn to counteract your negative emotions upfront, so these people can't use them against you. Don't make it so obvious how you feel. Don't wear your heart on your sleeve. This will help you make choices based on logic rather than of the moment. The goal is to consistently make rational decisions that result in positive emotions. Also stop being dependent on receiving approval. That's a really hard call because, of course, we all seek and need approbation at home and at work. We need to know that we are appreciated and that, as a person, we're OK. We need to know from others that we have value.

Much of the pain in our lives is the result of dependence. You depend on your boss (who may not, of course, be evil) for your income and livelihood, so you have to listen, say, to his incessant questions and answer him promptly, or he may make your life difficult or perhaps think less of you. You need to engage in some discussions about football, the weekend, his family, your family and so on. That's normal, of course. You also depend on your colleagues' sense of happiness and comfort, because if you don't keep them on the 'right' side, every day at the office will be miserable or uncomfortable. Who wants that? Our entire lives revolve around getting other people's approval. But the more we rely upon approval to feel positive about ourselves and the more we use approval as a benchmark for our happiness, the more we're likely to let other people control us.

To stop this vicious circle developing, begin by validating and checking yourself. Approve of yourself. Don't use other people's responses as a benchmark for success. Instead, develop a sense of confidence in yourself so that you always feel successful—so that you always have the energy you need to become more successful. Easier said than done? Of course it is, but the point is that you should take as much control over what happens to you as possible.

Never let your confidence levels be controlled by other people. Your manager comes into the office, asks you about a project or important task, you talk for a bit, he or she leaves and you feel good about yourself. You feel like you just got a little closer to your boss. You feel valued. You feel like your job is a little safer. Over time, your happiness and confidence become completely dependent on how many times your boss visits you. Or how many times he says something positive to you about your work. Or how many times he smiles at you. This is not to say that everyone is out to trap you. They are not. But if you are aware that things at work can be a tad tricksy from time to time, then some caution can't hurt. And tricksy doesn't mean evil. Seeking safety is just normal behaviour.

But, once again, any psychotic executive, one who has zero empathy for you or anyone else, is not going to allow you to be safe and, indeed, is unlikely to be helpful in your aim to be confident, because his role in your life is to take that away. You can deflect though, and you can try hard to remain impassive to his chipping away at your confidence. Confidence protects against dependency and control. Self pity saps it.

Confidence, of course, doesn't just happen. You have to develop it—and if you're feeling beaten, confidence will be in very short supply. Seek support from friends and family. Too many people fail to realize that confidence is an emotional state, like happiness, anger and sadness. And any victim of an evil executive is bound to feel unhappy, wretched, angry, frightened and enormously sad. If you have sufficient evidence of what's being done to you, if you have the law on your side and maybe union support too, then be confident. You may not have this job much longer (why would you want it?) but there's much more chance that senior people in your organization will need to sit up and take notice. But (and it's a big but) you must have everything in order so that your case is absolutely watertight. Cornered animals fight—and no less so, evil executives.

38

TYRANTS AND MACHIAVELLI

> ...the snares of watchful tyranny.
>
> *Macbeth*, Act V, Scene 8

The executive with tyrannical traits—oppressive, controlling and cruel—will resort to Machiavellian tactics and constantly make decisions that feed his ego. His primary concern is maintaining power and he will coerce and intimidate others to support him in that aim. The tyrant thinks of his subordinates or employees as rabble aboard his ship. He is the captain, he is the pirate and it is his ship. This is, however, not a Disney movie. Here the ending will doubtless be anything but happy.

The evil executive leads by fear. He classifies people in his mind and treats them accordingly, and anyone who challenges his thinking is treated as against him and as the enemy. Those who support his cause and achievements (usually gained through the efforts of others) with gestures of loyalty, find themselves in favour. Those who perform poorly, even though they are in the gang, become 'demoted' in the gang's food chain. Invariably it is these people who will betray others, lie and cheat in order to gain 'promotion' within the 'crew'. Sometimes it is people higher up the gang's hierarchy who smell power for themselves. Maybe they feel that they could be a better leader of the gang. Maybe they want some kind of revenge. Think Iago in *Othello*. Sometimes the evil executive discovers a 'plot' to oust him and deals (very firmly and sometimes finally) with the usurper, or engineers the removal of he who dares challenge his authority. The reality of scenarios like these, where ordinary folk trying to do a good job can see these machinations happening and the thought of the pain to come, can immobilise any decent person into abject terror and almost total inaction. Is this all an exaggeration? Well, it doesn't happen like this every day everywhere, but it happens.

Niccolo Machiavelli wrote his famous dissertation on power, *The Prince*, in 1513. His thoughts on the uses and application of power encompass every level, from proletariat struggles to strategies employed by monarchs in the 16th century. He discusses the necessity of cruel actions to keep power. He was unemotional in his desire to keep his lord and master safe and his position preserved. Emotion and kindness play no part. Machiavelli denied the relevance of morality in political affairs and held that any means and deceit are justified in pursuing and maintaining power. This definition implies that the end justifies the means. This is the core of Machiavellianism.

Well, it worked for Machiavelli, and it also works for executives with the desire to get their way, no matter what. The priority for someone who holds power is to maintain his position, regardless of the morality of the means. And at all costs. The evil executive knows that the best way to self-preservation is through power supported not necessarily by all the people, but by those who are good at doing the will of the protagonist—the toughs, the thugs, the guards, the acolytes, the gang.

Machiavelli doesn't preach evil per se. Essentially, he teaches how a prince should rule effectively in the face of challenges to stay in power. He maintains that atrocities are acceptable if they result in achieving the desired ends. However, gratuitous violence against the people under one's rule is unacceptable if this causes them to rebel against the ruler. That's a mixed message, of course, and an argument that justifies any action, evil or otherwise. Between being loved or feared, he chooses the latter, but also cautions against needless cruelty that results in enmity.

So, a painful but effective strategy with the tyrant is to present your ideas in a way that allows him to take partial credit. (He will, anyway.) The tyrant (aka evil executive) can then maintain his ego without having to shut down your idea. Always be quick to give him some credit, even though he is unlikely to reciprocate, because this will inevitably put you on his good side and he will in the future look to you for a repeat performance. However, don't overdo it and continue to try and be seen as one of his close buddies. You are not. Also, to survive a tyrant, you must choose your battles wisely. If you practise self-awareness and manage your emotions, you can rationally choose which battles are worth fighting and which ones you should avoid. Sometimes, you may not get to choose if the battle comes to you. Expect no real favours. Ever. This person is not your friend.

The goal is not to become an emotional punch bag. When the tyrant's mood pendulum swings to the dark side (and it will, often), be a sea of calm. You can't assume that he will settle down quickly, because he may not. His malicious, dark and ruinous mood may be prolonged. But, in any event, you help yourself and your health by being as relaxed and as 'in control' as possible.

The understandable reaction to anyone being consistently revolting to you is to either say nothing and suck it up, or to speak out—certainly at the beginning. Or suddenly, not being able to take any more, to lose control and shout and/or fight physically. You will undoubtedly lose out—and possibly lose your job, or certainly your pride and self-esteem. Indeed, matters will become worse and the jibes more frequent. Here's something to consider. Instead of tuning out the tirades, listen carefully to what the tyrant has to say. Many who stomp around angrily do so because they need to vent before they can discuss anything productively. Once the situation has calmed a little, try being empathetic. Then try and help the tyrant focus on core issues. If necessary, restate any problems he expresses so he knows that you are listening. Then communicate openly and be the voice of reason. None of these approaches are easy, so don't worry if they don't work. It is a truism that sociopaths and psychotics are likely to hold very little reason or logic, and therefore reason and logic don't stand much of a chance in conversations with them.

Be a beacon of honesty with the tyrant and indicate diplomatically that you would like to be given the same respect that you afford him. Admit to mistakes early. Put constructive criticism inside positive statements. This encourages good behaviour in return—even if it doesn't happen overnight or, possibly, at all.

39

INCOMPETENCE

> The fool doth think he is wise,
> but the wise man knows himself to be a fool.
>
> *As You Like It*, Act V, Scene 1

Many executives in organizations around the world are promoted for political reasons, hastily employed or hired haphazardly, and hold positions way beyond their capabilities. Most likely, an evil executive is not completely incompetent, but will have people who report to him who have been at the company a lot longer and have information and skills that he certainly lacks. This is how gangs work anywhere. The leader relies on information from 'trusted' lieutenants.

If you find yourself frustrated with this type of executive, it's probably because you have experience that he lacks or you know things that he simply does not. This is not unusual and does not make him evil. It is important to swallow your pride and share your experience and knowledge, without any arrogance or 'I'm smarter than you' attitude. Share the information that this person needs to grow into his role and you may become his ally and confidant. May. But with this comes strings, as we've seen. If you're his 'friend' you're in his coterie, and therefore he will have expectations of you, and want you to do things you may not like. Once 'in' the gang, it's hard to get out.

Some managers pretend. They pretend that they know how to manage. They pretend that they have experience. A pretender isn't always evil, but it is a characteristic of one who is. It's always a mystery how such bosses climb to their exalted posts. The Peter Principle pushed this point: that members of a hierarchy are promoted until they reach the level at which they are no longer competent. We've all seen examples of this. It's endemic in many organizations, although less so than it was when corporations allowed that kind of thing to exist. But downsizing and economies, as well as the need to streamline, have made the likelihood less frequent.

It's important that you are careful of your criticism of anyone who is seemingly incompetent. You can say, if asked, that someone doesn't have a good grasp of something. This is unemotional. Don't say something like, 'He's an A1 idiot who can't even tie his own shoelaces!' The former is verifiable; and while the latter may be true, it will come across as your jealousy of his position or income, not his lack of skill. Not least, the comment may well get back to the evil executive, and that bodes ill for you. But remember that incompetence, like stupidity, may just indicate that he's not very good at what he does. Keep in mind that doing is different from managing and being incompetent or weak at an aspect of any job absolutely does not an evil executive make.

You don't necessarily need to be able to do the work in order to manage those who do.

Smart bosses will, of course, give credit to their teams when things go well and take responsibility when they go badly. Praising a team shows that an executive is smart, not that he is stupid. Any organization will want to hire people who have built fabulous teams in the past, regardless of whether they can undertake specific tasks or not.

Incompetence is not unusual in organizations. Fact. Empathy is a huge part of what a decent manager offers a team. But we know that evil executives normally have no understanding of empathy. Managers are often faced with tough decisions that will negatively affect people and they make the best choice they can. But they can often forget to empathize with individuals or the team as a whole. They forget to explain their decisions, so that those negatively affected could better understand those decisions. They forget to involve those people in the decision in the first place, so that the people are active participants and not just victims. The failure to do this is a fast way to earn a reputation as an idiot, even if the intentions are solid. However, this behaviour is not evil, just incompetent.

There are always plenty of reasons not to take a decision, reasons to wait for more information, more options, more opinions, more reflection, more time—and this attitude can be a result of incompetence or the inability to manage. Quality leaders display a consistent bias for action. People who don't make mistakes generally don't do anything.

Legendary advertising guru David Ogilvy argued that a good decision today is worth far more than a perfect decision next month. People who prevaricate are usually not good leaders, but that does not make them evil.

Equally, love of procedure often masks a fatal inability to prioritize, or simply to do anything decisive—it's a bit like playing the fiddle while Rome burns. But, again, this is not evil, just poor management. As is the case of an executive who always produces the most perfect charts, forecasts and spreadsheets, who's always on time and who always volunteers for projects in which he has no core expertise. And does none of these things well. It's all displacement activity to hide the fact that he can't do his real job. This often happens, but it's not evil.

The manager who cannot set (and stick to) deadlines is usually found not to be able to manage, let alone honour commitments. A failure to set and meet deadlines also means that no one can ever feel a true sense of achievement with that person. Things are too loose, and most people don't like loose. You can't celebrate milestones if there aren't any. You can't manage achievement and you're never really sure when the job's done. This usually applies to anything that involves planning. Some managers love planning, but hate it when the planning comes to an end and the doing looms.

As indicated earlier, many evil executives hide behind a spurious track record, but this is not an attribute of evil executives alone. A common—but expensive—way to put off making decisions is to hire consultants who can recommend several alternatives. While others are figuring these out, the evil executive doesn't have to do anything. And when the consultants' choices are presented, the ensuing debates can often absorb hours, days and months. Meanwhile, your organization is poorer, but it isn't any smarter. When the consultants leave, they take your money and their expertise out of the door. In the case of the evil executive, the consultants' findings are often kept solely for the executive's use and can be a powerful weapon.

40

THE HIDDEN EVIL EXECUTIVE

> Thou poisonous slave,
> got by the devil himself.
> Upon thy wicked dam, come forth!
>
> *The Tempest*, Act I, Scene 2

To succeed with an antisocial, non team-playing, hide-away monster who only emerges from his room snarling, shrieking or accompanied by thugs, you need to speak his language. When you have an idea, make certain you have the precise data to back it up. The same goes for your performance—you need to know what he values and be able to show it to him if you want to prove your worth (even if you privately believe that your worth doesn't need proving). By the by, never assume that everyone agrees that you're smarter and cleverer than the tyrant. And you should never imply it either.

An important factor is when you begin trying to nudge the evil executive out of his antisocial comfort zone. The trick is to find ways to connect with him directly, without being pushy or rude. Schedule face-to-face meetings and respond to some of his emails by knocking on his door. Talking is, on the whole, better than emailing. Back up a conversation by email by all means but, just because you feel uneasy, don't avoid conversations. Many businesses run on email communication even when recipients and senders sit close to each other. Don't do that. It's pretty awful communications practice anyway. Forcing the tyrant to connect with you as a person will make him put a face to your name. Yes, of course that's possibly a double-edged sword, but let's be positive. Just because he's all about power and things other than you, it doesn't mean you can't take some advantage. Do so in small doses, however, because he's unlikely to respond well to the overbearing social type.

The executive in question may seem boring, slow and uninspired. He may also seem harmless, unchallenging and unworthy of attention. The tendency may be to ignore him or to patronize him for his antisocial behaviour. Be careful. And why patronize anyone, anyway? The executive may be quiet and evil, or he may be not quiet and evil; he may be loud, boorish, coarse and violent, even though he rarely emerges from his 'lair'.

Often these people are frightening, not just for obvious reasons, but because they react badly if cornered. They may need to have ideas explained to them to a very simple level, but get angry when this happens. They don't make instant associations and, when they do, they snap and become odious. And, as we've said, these people aren't usually stupid. They are often razor sharp. But talking to them about anything to do with future possibilities or anything logical is hard work. It's like holding a conversation with someone whose whole personality, culture and language are radically different from your own. You don't understand them, and they sure as hell don't get you. Or is it a front? Is it a guise so that you think they are stupid?

41

VISIONARIES

> I have had a most rare vision.
> I have had a dream, past the wit of man
> to say what dream it was.
>
> *A Midsummer Night's Dream*, Act IV, Scene 1

The evil executive's strength, you discover, lies in his ideas and innovations, often learned from books, the Internet, a previous employer or formal study. However, this quasi-entrepreneurial approach becomes dangerous when a plan or solution needs to be implemented and the evil executive can't bring himself to focus on the task at hand. When the time comes to execute his vision, he's already chasing the next idea and you're left to figure things out for yourself.

This kind of executive can use corporate (and any other) jargon well and can convince his bosses that he has vast and relevant experience for his current role. Usually he has neither. Or he might have both. Here is the chameleon—and you won't know until it's too late. The result is often all 'show' and this kind of executive does not, thankfully, last long. However, the time that he is within your orbit can be extraordinarily painful and damaging. Such an executive can fight like a mountain lion and will stop at very little to maintain his cover. If he believes that you are likely to expose him, then he will fight hard and dirty, particularly once the smoke and mirrors begin to fade.

To best deal with this type, reverse his train of thought. He naturally takes a broad perspective, so be quick to funnel things into something smaller and more practical. Do this by asking a lot of specific questions that force him to rationally approach the issue and to consider potential obstacles. Don't refute his ideas directly, or he will feel criticized; instead, focus his attention on what it will take to realistically implement his plan. Be wary of play-acting. Don't make anything up. Don't dissemble, even if that makes you feel better. He'll see through you in a heartbeat. Imagine that you're dealing with a snake, a large one that can move with lightning speed. One with fangs and venom.

One of the biggest problems here is that he and others like him will ask questions that are either impossible to answer (because the answer doesn't exist) or are unclear. The answer you give will be wrong, probably no matter what you say, and discussing the question can often lead to more confusion and ridicule.

Some evil executives love to push every latest piece of management hogwash at every meeting. They love phrases like, 'all-hands-on-deck' meetings and 'running' ideas up some particular 'flagpole'. They like to get some 'blue-sky thinking'. They want their people to be like 'SWAT teams', to be in the 'swim lane' and they like the idea of 'empowering' this and that. They refer to 'drinking the Kool-Aid', the 'bleeding edge', 'moving the needle', 'going forward' (please, no), the 'idea shower', 'looping back' and 'you can't turn a tanker around with a speedboat change'—and so it goes numbingly on. These are the executives who regularly read up on management tricks and sign up for one-day leadership boot camps, but fail to apply their learning for their employees' benefit. If in an office situation a staff member's behaviour doesn't align with one of their coveted social theories, they don't know how to react and dismiss it out of hand, usually by lashing out. Or they do react negatively on the basis that their 'visionary' thinking is the only view—period. These are the people who create PowerPoint decks that look good, but mean nothing. These are the people who choose style over content.

The modern workplace, where executives field last-minute requests, complaints and questions, where real issues are managed, where teamwork is encouraged and where challenges are met, is a good place to be. But it is difficult to support a scenario where an executive has his head in the clouds and becomes vitriolic with anyone who challenges his thinking. Challenge with care; you can do it through stealth, by offering practical ideas that begin to match the executive's thinking. Painfully slow, but a start.

42

RIGHT ABOUT EVERYTHING

> Come not between the dragon and his wrath.
>
> *King Lear*, Act I, Scene 1

We've all been there—sitting in the shadow of a manager who decided it was time to roll up his sleeves, swoop in and create a storm. Instead of taking the time to get the facts straight and work alongside the team to realize a viable solution, he deposits formulaic advice and then abruptly disappears, leaving everyone else behind to clean up the mess. These executives interact with their employees or colleagues only when there's a fire to put out. Even then, they move in and out so fast—and put so little thought into their approach—that they make bad situations worse by frustrating and alienating those who need them the most. What might have been a small fire with a smouldering twig or two suddenly becomes a huge conflagration.

What's more, they never accept blame and always seem to emerge with as the heroic leader who solved the problem, or, if the problem is not solved, as the person who recognized that someone else had caused the problem.

A group approach works best here. If you can get the entire team to sit down with the executive and explain that his abrupt approach to solving problems makes it difficult for everyone to perform at their best, this message is likely to be heard. Well, 'likely' is maybe too strong. If the entire group pulls together and provides constructive, non-threatening feedback, the executive may more often than not find a better way to work with that team.

Those who think that they're right about everything often do so because they unequivocally believe it—and evil executives are no different. It's a power play, obviously. It's more about the executive's level of anxiety and need to control situations, and the sense of control they get from feeling and knowing that they are right. It will have little to do with you per se. The bad news is that fighting back won't work. If you rebel against it, you're likely to get more of the same. So you can't change the way your boss is 'right all the time', but you can change the way you respond.

At one end of the spectrum you have managers who have very high standards and who like some degree of control. Why not? And they are (really) often right. They may regularly send you back to rework something that doesn't measure up. They pay a great deal of attention to detail and exercise some degree of control, but they don't stifle those who work for/with them. In fact, you may be able to learn a great deal from them.

At the other end of the spectrum are people best described as pathological, who need to make it clear to themselves and others that they are in control by declaring that they are in charge and are always right—and that no other opinion is valid. They are, like many evil executives, obsessive about power and, of course, control is vital for power. And they will insist that day is night—and insist that you believe it, too. If you push back by proving that the executive is wrong, or even less than absolutely right, then the heavens shall rain rocks. Instead, try to understand what is causing this person's behaviour. Is he under immense pressure? Is this his natural way of managing? Does the company culture encourage and reward this kind of approach?

It is likely that the executive has an outlook to which the world and its standards do not match up. You therefore need to make a conscious and honest effort to earn your manager's trust by succeeding in areas about which he cares. 'I see you're under unbelievable pressure. How can I help?' is a start. It may not work or he may tell you to disappear fast, but using a rich vernacular. However, it's worth a try. Or you could consider explaining the ideal plan of action and then ask for the executive's input. You could quote him. But don't stray into a topic where you could get lost. He'll see through you and he'll know his own game better than you.

Remember, then, that the 'always right' executive is often motivated by anxiety. He may be nervous about anyone else being able to do anything better than him. You can often address that concern by keeping him informed of a project's progress. You can schedule regular check-ins that help him feel a part of the process. Or you can send unprompted emails that share important information—unless his office is a few steps from yours, in which case try and tell him face to face and then support that with an email if required. If he has made it clear that he wants to know about detail, don't hesitate to get specific. If you quote facts, then make absolutely sure that they are right—always—giving the executive no room to gain or take an advantage. Don't hide behind anything. Don't say you know something if you don't. Once again, don't dissemble. Most importantly, if you have questions or need clarification, don't wait until the last minute, no matter how frightened you are.

43

THE INSULTING EXECUTIVE

> "A most notable coward, an infinite and endless liar, an hourly promise breaker, the owner of no one good quality."
>
> *All's Well That Ends Well*, Act III, Scene 6

Shakespeare wrote in *A Midsummer Night's Dream*, 'Tempt not too much the hatred of my spirit, for I am sick when I do look on thee.' He was adept at the clever insult, and each one offended at the right moment, had the desired effect, blocked a bully or saved an innocent who was in pain. Insults hurt, insults wound and they can have long-term and disastrous effects on an individual, causing prolonged mental anguish and worse. Again, this is not necessarily a sole characteristic of an evil executive. But, faced with an onslaught of insults, it is tough for you to take them. And why should you? Consider the female CEO who allegedly yelled at some executives she felt were underperforming: 'You're eunuchs! How can your wives stand you? You've got nothing between your legs!' Who knows if that's true, but we've probably all heard worse, and we've all probably witnessed the effect that targeted verbal attacks can have on people whether the comment focuses on body parts, religion, sex, abilities or whatever.

Feedback is necessary in any office and in any organization. A good executive will explain why you didn't meet expectations, as well as the changes he'd like to see next time. But then there's the other breed: the executive who doesn't only criticize your work, but who treats it with utter contempt and derision—and in so doing assassinates your character. The derision can be public and therefore doubly humiliating and it can allow others in the organization to take up the cudgel and beat you—very often for as long as you remain in that organization. Nicknames can accrue and not disappear. They are often not remotely funny but are, nine times out of ten, hurtful.

If the tyrant is not forthcoming about why he's not happy with you, you can take steps to prevent being berated. When you get an assignment, be sure you're crystal clear on the instructions before you start. That's important. If he still focuses his ire at you, and you don't know what you did to deserve it, take a deep breath and ask. You might want to wait until his tirade is over and his mood improves. Asking 'I'd like to understand where I fell short, so it doesn't happen again. Can you explain what you'd like me to do differently next time?' could clear the air.

Employees have a tough enough time finding their footing in an ever-changing workplace. The last thing they need is a leader who insults them by not having their best interests at heart and not appreciating their efforts. What to do when you're insulted repeatedly? It's important to deal with an insult immediately, otherwise the evil executive will do it again with impunity. He may do that anyway. And it's likely to get worse because he'll feel that he can do more without any impediment. But remove yourself from the situation before you do anything. Do not allow yourself to react without thinking through the other person's actions. If you do, you might say or do something in haste that you later regret.

Consider the nature of the insult. In the case of a mild one-off or very occasional insult, ignoring it is possibly the best course of action. Ignoring can help avoid making a small issue escalate to become a significant conflict. However, if someone openly insults you—in private or in front of others—and causes you distress and humiliation, you need to deal with it sooner or later, preferably sooner, so the person knows his behaviour is unacceptable. Serious insults, such as those accompanied by sexual harassment or intimidation and threats, should be handled immediately through the workplace chain of command. This may reap further taunts or worse, but that shouldn't diminish the need to do something. If the organization fails to act on your behalf and you can gain no traction through unions or law, then you need to seek a transfer or leave altogether.

If you think your judgment may be skewed, tell a trusted colleague about the insult and the circumstances surrounding it—and, anyway, it's a good idea to talk it through with someone you know you can trust. (Here's another 'on the other hand': in these situations betrayals are not unknown, alas.) Ask your confidant if s/he thinks you are overreacting to the evil executive's behaviour. Does it actually warrant further action? What action should you take, if any? An objective opinion can help you sort out your feelings and make the best decision when dealing with the insult. If the insult is not something you can ignore, but you don't feel you need to report it to a superior, deal with it yourself.

Ask the person who insulted you to meet with you in private. Don't talk to him in front of others, to avoid making him or indeed you feel uncomfortable. Use less confrontational 'I' statements instead of 'You' statements to explain how you feel about his insult. For example, say: 'I felt uncomfortable when my mistake was pointed out on the project in front of everyone the other day. I accept responsibility for that mistake, but we're supposed to be a team, and team members support each other.' Or: 'Look, I know I'm overweight. I'm trying hard to sort that out and it's difficult, so please don't make unpleasant and hurtful comments. Encourage me maybe?' These approaches may fall flat or on deaf ears; or the executive may, just may, admire your ability to be firm. Don't forget, though, that evil does not recognize the words 'understanding', 'empathy' or 'reason'. Being 'nice' isn't in his emotional vocabulary. Such a vocabulary is very limited.

It's a possibility (actually highly likely) that the person who insulted you won't acknowledge that his behaviour was unacceptable. If he won't apologize or verbally agree not to insult you again, let it go. The person now knows that you did not appreciate his remarks, and that was your goal. You may not reach a better conclusion. However, if it continues and becomes unbearable—and involves others—you absolutely must take the matter higher and further. Or go.

44

YOU'RE NEVER APPRECIATED

> Ingratitude is monstrous.
>
> *Coriolanus*, Act II, Scene 3

Sam Walton, founder of Wal-Mart, apparently said something along the lines of: 'Appreciate everything your associates do. Nothing else can quite substitute for a few well-chosen, well-timed, sincere words of praise. They're absolutely free and worth a fortune.' Well, it seems that Wal-Mart has not always stepped up to the plate on staff appreciation, and the same goes for many other organizations, but this sentiment from Sam is absolutely right. Donald Peterson, former chairman of Ford, said that the most important 10 minutes of his day were spent boosting the people around him. There are many, many examples of well-known executives and leaders who find staff appreciation and recognition absolutely critical to the success of their enterprise. It's not about staff being needy, but simply wanting to feel appreciated.

There are gradations, of course. There are few people who feel over-appreciated, but there are undeniably very many who feel under-appreciated—and some just not appreciated at all. If that is coupled with malicious behaviour that denigrates a person's abilities and makes them feel totally worthless, then the result is never going to be anything more than awful. We need praise at any age—it's a human need.

Appreciation makes us feel safe, whatever job we do and wherever we fit into society—it frees us to do our best work and be a better person. It's also energizing. When we feel undervalued, the worry and resentment generated can drain and divert our energy. But, praise has to be genuine. It can't just be thrown around willy-nilly, because then it has no value. You also need to trust the source of the praise. Do you admire and respect the giver? Do you think that he/she has understanding and empathy? Paranoia aside, if the praise is shallow and comes from a suspect source, you may find the result demotivating, cynical and part of a plan to unsettle you.

Consider your work environment. Remember that you have a job and praise, whilst good, needs to be deserved. Also, consider whether you are being treated in a different way from anyone else, and whether your colleagues are being treated in the same way as you.

Interestingly, many who expect praise give none or little themselves. So start appreciating others. Learn to give a compliment. Learn to take one. How many times have you caught yourself deflecting a compliment someone is giving you? All too often someone compliments us, and we shrug it off: 'It was nothing', we say, or 'Just doing my job.' We have to accept these kind words when given—even if they're a rarity.

Make your accomplishments known. Instead of directly confronting your boss about not feeling appreciated, find other ways to make him aware of your achievements. But don't overdo it. Nobody much likes a show-off. A subtle approach is always more effective than in-your-face self-promotion. Focus on benefits to the organization. Why wouldn't you? It isn't all about you.

Behind most good bosses is a good support team. Good managers recognize that they'd be beyond stuck if their staff abandoned them—and by that, take 'abandon' to mean not doing their work properly. Evil executives have a bad habit of starving their subordinates of praise. Praise where it's due—we all need it. The lack of praise doesn't automatically mean that a boss or executive is evil. However, if encouragement and praise are deliberately withheld in order to cause harm on a continual basis, then the repercussions can be damaging.

It's never fun to fish for compliments, but asking for feedback is necessary. Try: 'I'd really like to help make your job easier. Can you tell me how I'm doing that—and how I could do better?' He may call you a creep and he may not. Never underestimate the power of complimenting your boss—without, of course, being creepy. And this is not to say that like will always beget like, but offering support may help him feel better about you—which might be a key reason he's not comfortable praising you in the first place.

A good boss knows his success dovetails with making employees feel appreciated. A bad boss, however, claims your accomplishments as his own and will not offer praise. If you think he'd be receptive, you could try framing the conversation with your manager in a non-accusatory way: 'I'm really trying to get promoted this year, so it would be great if you could help me make others aware of my accomplishments—like that account I just helped win.' The downside (sorry) is that he may not want you promoted and he may want to claim the winning of an account as his very own. That happens too with managers who are just greedy and unfair, but not necessarily evil.

Be sure to put your feats in writing. If there's a way to claim credit for something you supported, led or achieved, let the rest of the team know before he has a chance to steal your thunder. But be careful. Even if you do this, the evil executive may still claim the credit, and in so doing discredit you no matter what you write, say or do. And, be careful not to fish for compliments for just doing your job. Not easy, is it?

One way to make sure your needs are met is to request a weekly one-to-one meeting with the executive. However, if you feel truly that you and your work are never appreciated, that you are criticized or are made to feel repeatedly useless, then knowing where you stand is very important. Demand an answer. Demand without yelling or threatening, but still be strong.

Another thing to consider is to seek out mentors in your organization, people with more experience or with different strengths from yours, and ask if they'll periodically offer you advice (maybe twice a month over coffee). Suggest this on a trial basis and if both parties aren't getting value after a month, agree to stop. Often there are experienced people, who aren't currently managing anyone, who will enjoy mentoring someone who is seeking guidance. This is beneficial anyway, because it will hopefully allow you to discuss the evil executive with someone else. But do be very, very wary. The person who is mentoring you may be a close colleague of the very person who is making you miserable.

You may have taken at least one personality test at some point in your career, such as: DiSC Profile, IDAK, Myers Briggs Type Indicator (MBTI), the MMPI and any number of tests based on the Five Factor Model of personality, such as the Revised NEO Personality Inventory. The presumption is that these personality tests include indicators that will identify individuals that are, or might be, toxic personalities; but unfortunately, in many cases, either these tests may unsurprisingly fall short, or toxic personalities are very clever at masking the results. Some specialists might be inclined to say that an executive is on the one hand 'toxic' but, on the other, 'nourishing', and that the same person has a good ability in getting along with other people, while another test may say the reverse.

One of the core concepts of tests like these is the contrast between toxic and nurturing behaviours. We may think of toxic people as those who consistently behave in ways that make other people feel devalued, inadequate, frustrated and guilty. In contrast, nurturing people consistently behave in ways that make other people feel valued, capable, wanted, respected and needed. Certainly, people do slip through any processing net and, as we've discussed, evil executives are shape-changers. They may appear one way at an interview and become something else further into their employment.

That is not to say that someone can do what Sauron does in J.R.R. Tolkien's Middle-earth novels. Sauron, the main antagonist of *The Lord of the Rings*, is a shapeshifter. Initially he can appear in any number of beautiful forms to deceive the gullible; and thus he forges the Rings of Power with the help of the Elves, who are deceived by his appearance. J.K. Rowling's *Harry Potter* series contains both Animagi, who can change to a single animal form and Metamorphmagi, who can alter their appearance. And in the movie *X-Men* the character Mystique/Raven is a blue female mutant who can transform into any sort of person; she can also change her voice. Well, to a degree this also happens in organizations. Many executives, some evil, are able to change manner, personality and behaviour in general, including their voice, to suit a set of circumstances. In addition, it's not unusual for people out for their own gain to say good things about an employee one minute and the reverse another.

45

EVIL'S SIGNATURE

> O, that way madness lies;
> let me shun that;
> No more of that.
>
> *King Lear*, Act III, Scene 4

It is possible that every organization contains at least one person whose difficult personality makes work more than just unpleasant for everyone around them. While this isn't universally true, it's very common. Working alongside difficult people is bad enough, but being managed by individuals with personality problems can be crushing. Of course, not everyone with a personality problem is a psychopath, and you mustn't jump to conclusions proactively. All that you can judge is how that person's behaviour affects you. Psychopaths and sociopaths can do extensive damage to colleagues and subordinates, often without personal consequences. Worse still, the very symptoms of the disorder seem sometimes to help them climb the corporate ladder.

'Psychopath' and 'sociopath' are words that have precise clinical definitions, but are often misused and overused. While Hannibal Lecter set the bar for the over-the-top, homicidal sociopath in *Silence of the Lambs*, the media noted at the time that these behaviours exist across a broad spectrum from acute to nearly undetectable. Even if you're not qualified to diagnose the condition clinically, sociopaths and psychopaths can usually be identified by their hallmark behaviour. There are several examples from movies, such as Norman Bates in *Psycho* and Gordon Gekko in *Wall Street*. Gekko is probably one of the most interesting, manipulative, psychopathic fictional characters. Hollywood has lately been fascinated by these successful psychopaths, in the wake of financial crises and high-profile trials such as Bernard Madoff's. Either way, the point is that any evil executive can be dangerous in some way.

Don't expect to spot a psychopath on first meeting. They are charming and, as often as not, bright and seemingly polite, fun and probably kind on the surface. We've noted that already. In casual conversation they will not blow their cover. Yet, if you're being managed by a psychopath, you'll probably discover that he lies subtly, often and successfully. In fact his skill at lying might be such that anyone may not even recognize the lies until after the conversation has long ended. Conversations may follow a path in a way that seems to bend reality and make others (maybe you) question what they (you) know to be true.

The best defence against lies is to preserve the truth in a form outside the psychopath's control. Keep (and perhaps even back up) all your emails, not least to be sure that something was agreed on a particular date or that you received an instruction in writing. Take notes for the same reason and to keep your memory refreshed. Whenever possible, make sure there are others present for all discussions. Don't be surprised when even the best-supported documentation fails against the evil executive's charm and clever deceptions. But you can at least make his more blatant lies, exaggerations, refutations or make-believe world harder to maintain.

It is critical to remember that sociopaths don't play by the same social rules that most people obey. In some sense, the sociopath believes that he has the right to behave in any way he chooses and that his social mores apply to him and nobody else. Therefore he feels no guilt or remorse for abusing, persecuting or otherwise taking serious advantage of anyone at any level—as long as he can get away with it. And he will try very hard to ensure that he does get away with it. At the same time, he can convincingly portray himself as a team player and pretend that he cares deeply for others. In order to maintain control, the psychopath may try to get close to a victim both physically (sexual harassment or even by demanding that his victim sit next to him in the office) and emotionally (making the victim cry, calling him/her extremely hurtful names, knowing which personal buttons to press, and so on).

The signs and symptoms of psychopathy—a heady mix of ruthlessness, fearlessness, charm, persuasiveness, egocentricity, impulsiveness and the absence of conscience or empathy—are terrifying. They will appear differently in different people and not always to the same extent or in the same mix. Organizations tend to be attracted to seemingly capable, intelligent, experienced people who ooze charm and charisma and seem to be able to persuade and influence others. As we've indicated already, at the outset these qualities are often mistaken for leadership or simply 'niceness' and capability, but as time goes on these people remorselessly manipulate their way into power. But remember, please, that not every successful, high-energy, intelligent, charming and persuasive person is a psychopath.

So, while he is usually supremely confident, bright, gregarious and tough, the evil executive is also a master manipulator and proficient at eliciting sympathy, compassion and empathy, which is curious since they give none of these things. On the other hand, they may be poor performers, and might frequently offer all kinds of circumstances that may explain to their managers why they are unable to achieve or deliver. We might feel sorry for them, and that's often the idea. Invariably they are excellent at diverting blame. They create smokescreens to divert attention. Moving people around, making unnecessary rearrangements of workspaces and office usage, imposing strange rules that have no perceived value, unsocial working hours, offering the promise of favours in return for telling tales on your peers, non-commitment to time-keeping, continual impatience—all can indicate psychopathic tendencies.

We assume that these people care about other people's feelings, because we do, because we assume that's what everyone does. Although they lack empathy, an evil executive will develop an actor's skill in evoking ours. He is likely to take you into his confidence, only to slowly suck out all of your ideas. He might confide in you about some simple or basic notion of his own (sometimes not yet fully formed), knowing that you are likely to improve on it. In a heartbeat, your idea becomes his and you won't get a look in.

Despite the fact that they may appear warm and friendly, psychopaths are completely self-centred, often matched by an arrogant and self-centred manner. The world exists for him. Friendships (if they can be called that) within the workplace are often terminated without warning once you or anyone else ceases to matter to the evil executive.

Psychopaths never accept responsibility for their mistakes and poor behaviour. It's always someone else's fault, and they can twist things so that it appears as if somebody else caused the problem in the first place. It can be easy for the evil executive to establish that this somebody else is very bad at his/her job or has not followed procedure. Worse than that, the evil executive is brilliant at manufacturing irrefutable evidence that makes someone else look guilty, so that the blame is deflected without fail—often with disastrous results for the falsely accused. The evil executive has no shame when it comes to using employees and colleagues as expendable buffers to maintain his own reputation. If his performance is questioned, he will have watertight believable responses which, when properly examined, carry no weight.

Things that would terrify most people don't seem to much frighten a psychopath. In fact, their composure in an emergency is part of their appeal, and explains why they often achieve success in highly volatile professions like the media, politics, finance and the military. But this lack of fear and perhaps misunderstanding of real risk can also lead to disgraceful comments, putting people in harm's way and other totally inappropriate behaviour. Power with impunity is what the evil executive wants. To achieve that, he will normally always try and impress those above by doing anything necessary (and whatever that may imply) to those below. Possibly psychopaths give out a certain aura, and a comment like 'He makes my skin crawl' speaks volumes. But not every psychopath will make anyone's skin crawl at the first meeting. Or at the second. Or at the third.

46

SAFETY

> And you all know, security
> Is mortals' chiefest enemy.
>
> *Macbeth*, Act III, Scene 5

Protecting yourself from attack, both emotionally and physically, must remain a priority. Daylight, witnesses, documentation, HR, unions, the law, friends and colleagues can be your allies. As the evil executive attempts to draw you closer, resist and create distance. Separate yourself physically as much as possible. If he pesters you with phone calls, let the calls ring to voicemail. Don't respond to emails immediately and check emails only at set times throughout the day. Be aware of your emotional tone when dealing with him. If you feel yourself becoming either too upset, angry or accommodating, either become much more neutral or bring the dialogue to a close as fast as you can. Most of us don't need to take phone calls at home or at weekends, so don't do it. It's better not to talk too much about your personal life; don't give anyone the opportunity of weaponry, at least until you know that someone very well.

Working with or for anybody who is bent on damaging you is totally debilitating and can ruin your health and your life. In the heat of being yelled at or in the most embarrassing of scenarios, difficult as it might be, try and remember that whatever the evil executive is saying, it is only his interpretation of the facts. Even if this ghastly individual has the power to dismiss you, he cannot take away your self-worth. It's important for all of us, in any role we have, to maintain friends and family who will hopefully help to ensure that we feel good about ourselves, our value and our worth.

One day, maybe long after you've left his orbit, this person may go too far. If he is caught red-handed in a clearly illegal or unethical act, with airtight proof, then a victim will have the upper hand, even though there may be some reluctance to use it. That's like turning the tables on the robber and holding the gun—he says 'Go on then, shoot.' And you can't. Nobody wants to be in that situation.

Use care when going over the evil executive's head since, as already argued, evil executives have been known to corrupt and co-opt managers above them. You might find yourself fighting against a unified management front. However, most HR departments do not want a lawsuit, so you'll likely find a more sympathetic ear there—but, sorry to say, not unequivocally. And, remember, don't make a complaint if it isn't properly valid or truthful; it'll probably backfire (quite rightly) on you.

Ultimately, no one ever deserves the abuse that evil executives hand out. As bad as the job market may be where you are, and as much as you've attempted to defend and protect yourself from the psychopath, retreat may be the only reasonable move. That isn't cowardice, not in any circumstances, and neither is it 'giving in'; it's protecting yourself. In the end, the evil executive's power to manipulate you, to harm you, is only as strong as your resolve to stay.

47

COMMUNICATE CLEARLY

> They have been at a great feast of languages and stol'n the scraps.
>
> *Love's Labour's Lost*, Act V, Scene 1

Consider when and how your evil executive likes to communicate. Don't give a long-winded report or essay if he wants a bullet-pointed status update on one sheet. If he gets angry at questions, try to soften those questions to ensure they don't sound critical. Don't ask questions for questions' sake. Seek his input and advice rather than sounding critical. Use words that he uses, but not over much because he'll think you're having a joke at his expense. Think about how he processes information. Does he prefer detail or an overview? How does he 'see' ideas? Basically, try and tune into how you believe he thinks and how he will react to whatever you're doing, saying or discussing.

In email correspondence really try hard and be crystal clear. Texts and emails have an unfortunate habit of being totally misunderstood. We can all attest to the fact that writing back-and-forth via email can become confusing, irrelevant and occasionally comedic. Try not to fill your executive's inbox with email after email from you. And also be conscious of what you decide to cc him. Some people refuse to acknowledge ccs, and if a line of email communication goes on and on, the growth of ccs along the way can irritate even the sanest. Only cc anyone where it really is important for the recipient to take note. If you expect action, then the email must be direct. That is courteous and avoids confusion. And avoid 'reply all' at all costs, unless it really is mission critical that 'all' need to read your reply.

Remember also that how you say something, the manner in which you say it and what you're communicating through your body language should also mirror the evil executive's style. Make eye contact as much as you can and lean forward to show engagement, but try not to take an overly aggressive posture. Of course, none of this is easy when you're in the middle of a terrible situation and an environment of constant fear; any advice seems impossible to put into practice. But keep going.

Be polite, but assertive. If you work for an overbearing taskmaster who deliberately gives you an unreasonable amount of work, try saying: 'Thank you for assigning me these projects. I'm also working on a number of other urgent ones for you. Because I won't be able to get everything done this week, how would you prioritize them?' If you are unclear as to the task being set, ask questions immediately that will help you to absolutely understand what you are expected to achieve and by when, but also questions that will potentially help the executive to articulate his own expectations: 'When do you need the proposal? About how many pages are you thinking? Similar to the last one?' Of course, you may not receive a reasonable reply. Or a reply at all.

Each executive, evil or otherwise, has his own communication style. You too. To be an efficient communicator, you must realize that communication is about both you and the other person. To improve communication, pay attention to the executive's preferred method and style. Listen carefully. When someone is abusive, it is very hard to decipher what is meaningful information and what is just noise and invective. When in doubt, don't be afraid to ask. The first rule in communication is to be an active listener. Instead of worrying about what you are going to say next, pay attention and listen to what the other person says. Good listening skills may help you understand and anticipate an evil executive's needs. Have a notepad handy. By taking notes, you will remember more of the conversation.

The executive will believe that his time is valuable. Well, it may be, or it may not be. Assume that it is. Pay attention to his schedule and don't try to communicate when he's under a deadline or is dealing with something urgent. If what you have to communicate is critical to the completion of a current project, be succinct and to the point. Get to the point of the discussion first and then go backwards if questions are posed. This will keep your communication streamlined and focused.

While emotion does creep into the business environment, make it a point to keep emotion out of discussions you have with anyone, the evil executive included. Maintain an even and professional tone throughout, if you can. If you need to communicate with him about a personal problem (not the best choice, since it may be used against you), a problem with a co-worker or some other issue that causes you to feel emotional, wait until you are clear-headed and as unemotional as possible before attempting to discuss or explain it.

Fearful as you may understandably be, don't run away and hide when a problem pops up or a mistake occurs. Respond to it proactively and don't keep the evil executive in the dark. Communicate your own proposed solutions so that you have a platform on which to start a problem-solving conversation. Explain the 'bottom line', whatever that may mean in the context of your proposition. If you need something, be specific. Saying 'I need help' is undefined. More defined is, 'I need Emma to help for four hours on this project.'

Once the executive has agreed to your proposal, leave the meeting if possible or move on to another topic. Don't give him the opportunity to change his mind. Similarly, you need to be aware that your proposal or recommendation for action may be the best solution given the information you have, but it may not be the best solution overall. The executive may have additional information or political battles to fight that do not have to be explained to you there and then, or indeed at all. (On the other hand, it would be very easy for him to rubbish your proposals and hide behind the pretence of additional information or political considerations.)

A point of caution (yes, another one)—you may not like it, but there is some truth in the feedback you may call criticism. Use the feedback to devise solutions and not to offer excuses. Even if you think you are in the right, your message is possibly not getting communicated to the executive clearly. If you do the right thing, that's more or less all that counts, whatever the outcome.

48

PLAYING POLITICS

> Something is rotten in
> the state of Denmark.
>
> *Hamlet*, Act I, Scene 4

You know that going over your boss's head to his boss can be dangerous. If you feel you must go over his head, then make sure you tell your boss about what you are doing—and that's not going to be remotely easy, is it?

Office politics is not about the normal disagreements and squabbles that inevitably arise when groups of people interact at relatively close quarters over a period of time. It isn't about the colleague who plays the radio too loud, the woman who insists on telling you about her date last night or the man who takes umpteen coffee breaks every day and tells you in lurid detail about the latest happenings in the world of a particular TV soap. And neither is it about flattering your boss, agreeing with everyone come what may or retreating into a shell and not offering any input into decision-making if asked.

Office politics is about knowing who holds the power—the people who carry most weight and influence at all levels—and how to get things done. Office politics is about understanding management styles and behaviours, who does what, and understanding how to interact with personalities. Most executives and managers have favourites—favourite employees, favourite ideas and favourite ways of dealing with peers and subordinates. It's all very challenging and by no means always clear.

In navigating office politics, it's vital to observe, listen and read what superiors do and say, how they operate and what they expect. That's all normal but it's not easy and will take time. It's also important to understand how management makes its decisions, how decisions are announced, what they want to achieve and, most importantly, how those instructions impact you. Another thing: enquire about executives who have something of a reputation. If there is a known evil executive in the workplace and he hasn't had any connection with you (yet), find out what he does and how, what makes him angry and who his targets/victims are. Be very careful, though. Those whom you ask might tell him, and then you can become a target. If you're new to the workplace, watch and listen a lot. Do not pass judgments, even if asked. Keep a low profile. Listen rather than speak. A simple mistake can make enemies. Be careful not to side with anyone overtly, but don't be afraid to disagree, as long as you have proof and facts. But disagree politely.

As important as it is to know the ins and outs of office politics, it is also important to know what they are not, as this will possibly keep you out of trouble. Office gossip, water-cooler chats, after-work drinks, hushed conversations—these aren't office politics. It is none of your business what any employee does with his or her personal time, who they're dating or who got in trouble. Stay away from this kind of thing. Petty squabbles—such as whose desk or cubicle is bigger, who has a better computer or set of tools, who came in late yesterday or who isn't pulling his or her weight—are not your business either, unless they involve your direct reports or have some close effect on your own performance. And be very careful at an office celebration or work function, particularly when alcohol is involved. Be careful what you say and be careful not to take onboard too much chitter-chatter and jibber-jabber. Don't drink too much, even if others do. Enjoy yourself, but remember your responsibilities and also be wary of false friends.

Office politics can, of course, be used by the malicious executive. Power and networking within a corporation can be used to gain some benefit to achieve his objectives. This often involves (for starters) game-playing, manipulation and malicious gossip. The politically astute evil executive will possibly size you up and see what sort of character you are. He will have knowledge of the formal and informal decision-making process in his section, team or the whole organization. He will know how to use the system to his advantage—and he will do just that. He will be able to identify the key players at all levels and he will know their strengths, weaknesses, likes, dislikes, hidden agendas, and the amount of power or clout they wield.

Over time, wherever you fit into the company, business, team, organization or whatever it is that you're in, by properly navigating the landscape of the local or 'global' politics, you will show that you understand the culture. One of the biggest consequences of office politics is that the individuals who are best at doing an actual job are often overlooked. Instead, office politics can reward individuals who are just OK at their job but great at playing political games. Just like every other game, there will be a winner and a loser, and this game may be dangerous, particularly when the games master is a tyrant.

49

THE END

> Farewell! God knows when we shall meet again.
> I have a faint cold fear thrills through my veins,
> That almost freezes up the heat of life.
>
> *Romeo and Juliet*, Act IV, Scene 3

First, consider that you can't change the evil executive. For whatever reason, he (or let's be honest, she) is unable to lead, manage, produce, deliver and so on. But he is also violent, psychotic, dangerous, harmful—and will think nothing of destroying anything or anyone who gets in his way. Yet, as discussed, the reality is that many organizations in every walk of educational, business and political life keep and reward evil executives. You can only control how you respond to any threat or harm. Don't allow yourself to be a victim—if you do, sooner or later you must leave. You may want or need to leave anyway. You spend too much time at work to let an evil executive ruin your career or life.

You must start to handle a threat by working on yourself first. Centre yourself by doing an honest self-inventory about your strengths and any areas needing improvement. All of us need some improvement, so don't balk at that. Be very sure that whatever is upsetting you is not because of you or something *you're* doing. If possible, ask someone you trust at work to assess you truthfully. Ask the evil executive for a meeting to clarify his expectations. Create a plan, with goals and action steps. Then present it and ask for input. Listen and make appropriate adjustments. Why will this help? You are trying to minimize misunderstandings about what has to be done and why. The evil executive may be pleased with your initiative, sparing him that necessity. Or he may not, of course. Remember you're dealing with someone who has few or no feelings and is highly unpredictable.

Most cynical evil executives hate surprises, unless they are of their own making. Let yours know what's going on—through email, meetings, casual or formal updates. However, don't overdo it. Learn the timing and process that seems to work best for him. By doing this, you will also learn other information that will help you to help him look good. Why is this useful? This isn't crawling. You are specifically checking in to keep your boss off your back and to make an already tough situation better for you. A common mistake in dealing with bad bosses is avoiding or retreating from them. This will just add to your trouble.

Be principled, but don't be stupid. If you fight a bad boss on everything, you most likely will lose and probably exhaust yourself in the process. Many victims of evil at work end up mentally and physically exhausted. He will know this, and he will see the exhaustion as a weakness. Pick your fights carefully. Don't confront, but instead discuss—if you can. It's unlikely that you'll win a confrontation, but that doesn't mean you should shy away from addressing something. Be as positive as possible by employing facts and plans to support your point of view. Document your concerns. You may (stress may) gain his respect and you may maintain your integrity.

Discreetly talk to other people with whom you work. How do they experience the executive? Is it just you? How do others deal with him? As mentioned, you may consider talking to the evil executive's boss. But be careful. This may backfire. First, research the status of their relationship. What kind of leader is the executive's boss? Is she/he like your executive, or is this person approachable? Going over your executive's head could come back to haunt you big time.

Contact HR if nothing seems to get better. Again, as mentioned, you have to gauge the type of HR team you have. Are the people compliance-driven, or are they employee advocates? Will they take the side of the person against whom you want to complain? Will they give some helpful counsel to you while they investigate and keep your comments anonymous? Some organizations have employee hotlines coordinated through HR. Research that option. But you can't begin a complaints procedure just because you're having a lousy week—unless, by 'lousy', that clearly involves some of the evil that we have discussed. Just having a busy, stressful, difficult, tiring week doesn't cut it. We all have those.

If you do decide to contact HR, take someone else with you who can corroborate your complaint and who knows some, if not all, of the detail. You're also less likely to be dismissed as a whiner (or retaliated against) if others support what you have to say. But that's not guaranteed, either. Again, document everything if you can. You need evidence for your claim that the evil executive's actions, behaviour and attitudes are affecting your health, your safety and your ability to work beneficially for the organization. It should be to the organization's advantage, of course, to resolve conflict whenever possible because, in the long run, low morale, a dark, hostile work environment and high turnover are costly. Unfortunately, what should be in an organization's best interests according to you are not necessarily the same interests according to others.

Let's suppose you do all the right things and nothing changes. Chronic stress will undeniably and eventually make you ill. So, leave. Get out.

50

AND IF YOU CAN'T EASILY GET OUT...

> And we must take the
> current when it serves,
> Or lose our ventures.
>
> *Julius Caesar*, Act IV, Scene 3

If you're in no position to quit, or if you don't have the luxury of just walking away, even if it's making you ill or desperately unhappy, there are a few things you can do, at least in the short term. First and foremost, try and find co-workers who'll watch your back. This can be difficult if your co-workers are guilty of terrible behaviour in their own right, but if you can rally a few, it's a good idea. When one of you hears something that'll impact everyone, like some big change that's about to sweep the department or a new policy that will affect how you do things on the shop floor, you can all share that information and try and protect yourselves. It's all about being on the same side and helping one another. Feeling that you're not alone is a good feeling—if it's real. Nurture that.

Ignore caustic groups. They are usually toxic, and unfortunately toxicity breeds more of the same and worse.

Sometimes, the best thing to do is to make absolutely sure you know who your friends or supporters are (not always easy and, let's face it, there may be none) and keep a low profile as much as possible. But don't look beaten or frightened. In the end, sometimes you are indeed on your own—and then you simply have to consider leaving.

Good relationships (at work certainly, but actually anywhere) are built on trust and, if there's no trust where you work, the only person you can depend on is you. Keep all of your various documents and emails organized. Hard, perhaps, but if you're in a toxic scenario you need to protect yourself. That way, if anyone tries to go back on their word, you can pull out an email or document where they said otherwise; or if a manager tries to pretend his policy says one thing when it really doesn't, you have some proof. This doesn't always work. The evil executive will fight and will know numerous ways and methods of tripping you up, so tread carefully.

You could try and get moved to another unit, department or division. That may work, provided that the evil executive doesn't have acolytes there, too. You can ask for a transfer to another building or another factory if the organization is large. You could try and seek redress through the law, but that can be costly and time-consuming. And you may not win.

While you have a modicum of sense left and you are sure that things won't improve, then it really is probably best to go. The last interview in Part One of this book told the tale of slavery. Well, those people can't get out—but you probably can. It may be the only way and you may look back and consider it the best move you could have ever made.

POSTSCRIPT

> If you can look into the seeds of time,
> And say which grain will grow and which will not,
> Speak then to me, who neither beg nor fear
> Your favours nor your hate.
>
> *Macbeth*, Act I, Scene 3

As much as it would be good to say that toxic work environments aren't about being personal, in many cases, they absolutely are. Sometimes an evil manager may have it in for you or just want to make you a convenient scapegoat for his own incompetence. Maybe you're today's target. Or tomorrow's. Maybe you did something innocuous that he has decided deserves huge punishment. Maybe, as we've noted, you're the 'wrong' religion, colour or shape. He may think that you're a soft target precisely because of your sex, size, creed, language, accent, preferences, hairstyle—anything physical or social. Whatever it is, it will be personal and enormously painful. Remember though, while it may be personal, it's not likely to be your fault. If it is, then consider what you can do to redress the situation, but don't accept blame where blame is unreasonable or downright wrong.

Don't let yourself get caught up in the swirl of negativity that is likely to surround a toxic situation. Remember, the goal is to get your work done so that you can leave satisfied at the end of the day, so you really don't want to go looking for confrontation. However, if it finds you, don't back down or roll over. You don't want others to get the message that they can regularly pick on you, make you a scapegoat and blame their mistakes on you, without you standing up for yourself. Pick your battles wisely though, don't put yourself in the way of harm or danger, but don't let personal slights and workplace confrontation go unchallenged.

Remember that every job is a two-way street: the job or the organization should need you as much as you need it; if you get the feeling you need it more than the organization needs you, it's time to balance the ratio or move on. There's no usual reason to keep working in a place where people don't respect or appreciate you and, worse, show that they don't.

It's important to realize that you cannot control what other people say and do. You cannot. You might influence people, but that's all. You can only control your own actions and reactions. This realization will allow you to let go of owning other people's negative behaviour and will empower you to focus on improving yourself and making changes that you want, not ones that others dictate. We can all make changes, even if they are modest. Yes, of course it's not easy to run off and find another job, but if your environment is so toxic and unbearable, then you simply must.

Never sacrifice your personal integrity in an attempt to get revenge or fight fire with fire. That's not easy, because revenge is a comforting thought, especially if we are desperately unhappy or very angry. Toxic work environments come and go; if you can learn something from this kind of situation, great. But as long as you're in it, watch your back and keep your profile low until the smoke clears, if it ever does—or get out. And then breathe clear and clean air.

Evil executives make people's lives a misery. They make people run scared. On occasion they cause the end of people's lives. They put people in a defensive mode, which interferes with an organization's ability to generate innovation and positive action.

According to American super salesman and author Zig Ziglar, 'Workers have three prime needs: interesting work, recognition for doing a good job, and being let in on things that are going on in the company.' Authors Leigh Branham and Mark Hirschfeld also wrote: 'It's sad, really, how a negative workplace can impact our lives and the way we feel about ourselves. The situation is reaching pandemic heights—most people go to work at jobs they dislike, supervised by people who don't care about them, and directed by senior leaders who are often clueless about where to take the company.'

A final point: make sure that you don't find the lure of evil exciting and something to embrace. Don't join in because you can—or because it's easy, or because you feel pressured to join. You are you. Don't become an evil executive.

Ernest Hemingway wrote in *Islands in the Stream*: 'Being against evil doesn't make you good. Tonight I was against it and then I was evil myself. I could feel it coming just like a tide... I just want to destroy them. But when you start taking pleasure in it you are awfully close to the thing you're fighting.' And Abraham Lincoln put it well, too: 'I would rather be a little nobody, then to be an evil somebody.' Don't be an evil somebody. You also have no need to be a little nobody, but that's a whole different book.

Simon Maier
London, 2016

ABOUT THE AUTHOR

Simon Maier has been involved in events and corporate communications for over 25 years and also has huge experience in—and a recognized reputation for—creating and directing worldwide corporate, public, televisual and commercial events. He has also in his time led a number of international communication agencies and consulted directly with businesses and governments on how to achieve good results from their communication strategies, some of which he devised.

Simon has always been fascinated by leadership and what makes a brilliant business or political leader, along with how leaders successfully engage their internal and external audiences. He is particularly interested in presentation techniques, speeches, styles and stagecraft. In equal measure, he has long been intrigued as to how and why some managers cause terrible harm to people and, eventually, to the organizations for which they work. 'Bullying in organizations worldwide is endemic,' he says, 'but, sometimes, and more often now, there are cases where actions by some executives can be said to be much more than bullying—and are examples of pure evil.'

Simon regularly presents to organizations on communication and how barriers to its success can be overcome. He acts as a business therapist to a number of organizations and helps employee groups and sales-forces change their mindsets from negative to highly positive.

His great love is theatre, particularly Shakespeare, and indeed he began his career in lecturing on Shakespeare at university level both in the UK and the U.S.

Other books from Simon's pen include: *The 100: Insights and Lessons from 100 of the Greatest Speeches Ever Delivered*; *Inspire!: Insights and Lessons from 100 of the Greatest Speeches from Film and Theatre*; *Speak Like a President: How to Inspire and Engage People with Your Words*; *The Diary: 100 Days and Lessons in Corporate Communications*; and *In Any Event: Top Tips on Managing any Corporate Event.*